IT HAPPENED IN COLORADO

By James A. Crutchfield

Illustrated by Lisa Harvey

TWODOT

To Mary and Harvill,
with love and appreciation

7 8 9 10 MG 03 02 01 00

The publisher gratefully acknowledges the assistance of Liston Leyendecker, Professor of History, Colorado State University.

The author would like to thank Roger Fletcher for permission to use excerpts from *The Wetherills of the Mesa Verde*, by Maurine S. Fletcher.

Crutchfield, James Andrew,   1938—
       It happened in Colorado / by James A. Crutchfield ; Illustrations by Lisa Harvey.
       p.   cm.
ISBN 1-56044-364-2 (pbk.) : $8.95
       1. Colorado—History—Anecdotes. 2. Colorado—History—Miscellanea.   I. Title.
F776.6.C78 1993
978.8-dc20   92-55079
                                                                  CIP   ·

Falcon® Publishing, Inc.
P.O. Box 1718, Helena, MT 59624

Preface

This book highlights thirty-four interesting episodes of Colorado history, from prehistoric through modern times. Each story is complete in itself and can be read individually and out of sequence.

Colorado is an extremely important state historically, and although the vignettes in this book do not in any way purport to comprise a thorough history of the state, they have been chosen selectively to give the reader an understanding of the broad historical background of the Centennial State.

I hope that *It Happened in Colorado* will provide a few hours of pleasure to those who read it, and that it will perhaps find its way into the classrooms of the state, thereby giving younger generations a better appreciation of their vast heritage.

James A. Crutchfield

Contents

CHAPTER ONE

THE GREAT
BUFFALO HUNT
· 6,500 B.C. ·

The band numbered about one hundred people, mostly men and women, but a small group of older children tagged along as well. The younger tots had been left with a few women at a temporary campsite two miles away. The day was warm and dry, typical of early fall on what would someday be the southeastern Colorado plains. But to the men and women of the group, the weather was not important, for today they hunted bison. Everyone knew that before the sun vanished in the western sky, they would have part of the meat and hides necessary to feed and clothe them during the coming winter.

The people were not native to these environs. They had marched across the dry prairie from the east, specifically to hunt bison. They called no place home but moved about constantly instead, following the game animals that provided them with food and the materials for shelter.

The horse, although originally native to North America, had already become extinct here and would not be reintroduced by the Europeans for more than eight thousand years. Consequently, these natives, members of the culture that archaeologists call "Paleo," traveled on foot, accompanied only by their ever-present dogs. The people were armed with spears and skinning knives. The bow and arrow had not yet found their way to the New World.

The day before, a couple of scouts had brought news of a bison herd's approach. The excited pair had run into the small camp and hastily conferred with their leaders. They told the chiefs that they had seen a herd of about two hundred bison traveling in almost a straight line directly toward camp. The scouts had left the herd about twenty miles away, and they figured by about noon tomorrow the bison should be nearing the little creek that passed nearby. They knew from experience that the great shaggy beasts would spend the day drinking from the stream, one of the few sources of fresh water for miles around.

The scouts also brought news that they had discovered, about two miles upstream from camp, a small arroyo that led from the elevated plain down to the creek. The arroyo was actually a beaten path, made over hundreds of years by bison running down the slope toward the precious water. Where the ravine approached the creek bank, it was nearly twelve feet wide and seven feet deep. After considering the possibility of ambushing the bison near the arroyo and stampeding them over the steep precipice, the hunters decided they could kill many more animals this way than by attacking the herd one bison at a time.

It was about noon when the hunters saw a cloud of dust on

the horizon that told them the bison herd was drawing near. Scattering about the head of the arroyo, the men and women found hiding places behind clumps of tall prairie grass and waited. Fate was with them, for the wind was right, blowing toward them from the direction of their prey.

Soon they heard a rumbling sound. The earth shook, and they knew that the animals, sensing the presence of water, were moving faster. The bison made a beeline for the head of the arroyo, which was little more than a depression in the ground. Faster, faster the herd moved. As the thirsty animals were about to enter the ravine, the hunters rose from their hiding places, waved buffalo robes, and made all the noise they could.

The frantic bison turned toward the creek, but several hunters rose out of the grass and turned them directly toward the middle of the ravine. As the lead animals approached the gulch, they did not see that they were about to step into an abyss until it was too late. The animals crowding behind them pushed them off the precipice before joining them in a mass of broken bones and bleeding bodies on the floor of the ravine. More hunters, concealed along the opposite bank of the gulch, jumped into the vast pile of animal flesh below and finished off any survivors with their spears. It was all over in a matter of minutes.

It was a good hunt. Nearly all of the two hundred animals lay dead on the floor of the arroyo. By day's end, the women had skinned and butchered most of them. They left untouched the few animals that were first to go over the edge, since those had been crushed beneath the more recent casualties.

Archaeologists estimate that this ancient bison kill, which actually occurred nearly 8,500 years ago near Big Sandy Creek in southeastern Colorado, yielded close to 57,000 pounds of meat and ten thousand pounds of fat and organs, plus scores of hides. And if these prehistoric tribesmen were anything like the more recent Plains Indians, they also made use of many of the bones, ligaments, and other body parts of the versatile bison.

The Big Sandy Creek site was discovered by amateur archaeologists in 1957. Today, it remains one of the most important examples of the ingenuity of America's early inhabitants. The bison kill was no accident. It was the product of planning, extensive knowledge of the bison's habits, and group cooperation. In years to come, Plains Indians would use a similar technique to slaughter hundreds of bison at a time.

CHAPTER TWO

THE DOMINGUEZ-ESCALANTE EXPEDITION

·1776·

On July 4, 1776, the Declaration of Independence was approved by the Continental Congress in Philadelphia. And in the faraway Spanish town of Santa Fe, two men planned to leave that day on an expedition that was bound for Monterey, California, and back again.

As events turned out, the pair did not begin their journey until July 29. It was early in the morning when the peaceful party of ten men left the plaza at Santa Fe "without noise of arms" and with the hope that "God will facilitate our passage as far as befits His honor, glory, and the fulfillment of the will of the All High that all men be saved." Before returning to Santa Fe on January 2, 1777, they would travel through more than two thousand miles of wilderness in today's states of Colorado, Utah, Arizona, and New Mexico.

The two leaders of the expedition were Francisco Atanasio Dominguez, a thirty-six-year-old Franciscan missionary, and Francisco Silvestre Velez de Escalante, a Franciscan friar who was about ten years younger. For several months prior to his journey, Escalante had been a missionary at both Laguna Pueblo and Zuni. Dominguez had also visited among various Pueblo tribes, having been sent by his superiors in Mexico City to inspect and document the lands of northern New Spain.

It was an odd assemblage that left Santa Fe that July morning. In addition to the two Franciscan friars, there was an astronomer/ cartographer, a chief guide and interpreter, a magistrate from Zuni, a blacksmith, and four others. In addition to the horses they rode, the men were accompanied by extra mounts, pack mules, and cattle.

The first few days of travel were uneventful. Crossing the Rio Grande at Santa Clara Pueblo, the expedition made its way northwestward. It crossed the Chama River on August 1. Continuing in the same general direction, it reached the present-day Colorado border on August 5. Crossing the San Juan River near the lost town of Carracas, close to today's Navajo State Recreation Area, the Dominguez-Escalante party entered Colorado.

In the vicinity of today's Navajo Reservoir, just a few miles from the border crossing, the Spanish friars found the terrain to their liking. Escalante wrote in his journal that

> there is good land, with facilities for irrigation and everything else necessary for three or four settlements, even though they might be large ones.... there are dense and shady groves of white cottonwood, dwarf oak, chokeberry, manzanita, lemita, and garambullo. There is also some sarsaparilla, and a tree which looked to us like the walnut.

Today, this area of southwestern Colorado lies beneath Navajo Reservoir.

Continuing to the northwest on August 7, the expedition soon crossed the Piedra River. Later in the evening, the men made camp on the banks of the Los Pinos River near today's town of Ignacio. They were now in Ute Indian country.

The following day, the small party of Spaniards crossed the Florida River near present-day Oxford and camped for the night on the Animas River near today's Durango. On the ninth,

Escalante found the land between the Animas and La Plata rivers to be

> very moist, for because of the nearness of the sierra it rains very frequently. For this reason, in the forests, which consist of very tall straight pines, small oaks and several kinds of wild fruits, as well as in its valleys, there are the finest of pastures. The climate here is excessively cold even in the months of July and August.

Continuing its journey, the Dominguez-Escalante Expedition passed the present-day towns of Mancos and Dolores. The Spaniards were only a few miles from Mesa Verde, but neither friar mentioned the cliff dwellings that were found there a little more than one hundred years later.

Just beyond Dolores, the men came upon "a small settlement of the same form as those of the Indians of New Mexico, as is shown by the ruins which we purposely examined." Today, these ruins of the Anasazi culture, occupied around A.D. 900, are part of the Escalante Ruins Historic Site northwest of Dolores.

By about August 16, the explorers were in the neighborhood of present-day Egnar. Turning northeastward from there, they continued past today's towns of Naturita, Nucla, and Montrose. From Montrose, the friars took a "backward S" route past Olathe, Paonia, Bowie, and Collbran. They crossed the Colorado River near Grand Valley and continued down Douglas Creek to its confluence with the White River, where they camped in early September.

Along Douglas Creek, Escalante wrote, "we saw crudely painted three shields... and the blade of a lance. Farther down on the north side we saw another painting which crudely represented two men fighting." This was the artwork of people of the Fremont culture, who had inhabited the region from around A.D. 700 until the mid-1100s. On about September 10 or 11, the two friars and their little party crossed from Colorado into Utah.

The Dominguez-Escalante Expedition never got as far as Monterey. By the time it arrived back in Santa Fe, after a circuitous trip through Utah and northeastern Arizona, the group had traveled over much of the Great Basin without getting near the Pacific Ocean. The party had journeyed into regions never before seen by white men. They had encountered Indian tribes unknown to their superiors back in New Spain. And although the mission was technically a failure, the two humble friars accomplished a monumental journey of discovery, making the trip peacefully and "without noise of arms."

CHAPTER THREE

ZEBULON PIKE'S ESPIONAGE MISSION
• 1807 •

"What, is not this the Red River?" exclaimed Lieutenant Zebulon Pike, as a company of Spanish cavalry approached him along the headwaters of the Rio Grande. It was February 26, 1807, and Pike and his command were more than seven months out of St. Louis on a mission that ostensibly was to take them to the headwaters of the mysterious Red River.

But Pike and everyone in his party knew that they were nowhere near the Red and that, in fact, they were well across the American border and deep within Spanish territory. When the Spanish captain politely offered to equip Pike and the others with mules, take them to the source of the Red River, and point them toward home, Pike refused.

Why would the lieutenant reject such a generous offer when by accepting it he would not only fulfill his mission to the letter but be on his way home after a grueling winter in the Rocky Mountains? To find the answer to that question, one must explore the motives of the organizer of Pike's expedition, General James Wilkinson. Already the highest ranking U.S. general, Wilkinson was given in 1805 the additional responsibility of governing the recently purchased territory of Louisiana. The appointment gave Wilkinson the perfect opportunity to put into action a plan he had been nurturing for some time: the establishment, with the help of Aaron Burr, of a southwestern empire.

General Wilkinson was a double agent. He served both the United States and Spain, and for years he had been conferring with Spanish authorities about the possibility of creating a Spanish-American government in which he and Burr would be the kingpins. It was with this thought that the governor/general sent Zebulon Pike west with the reported goal of finding the source of the Red River. Actually, Wilkinson wanted him to spy out the Spanish territories and towns of the Southwest.

Pike and twenty-three men left St. Louis on July 15, 1806. They ascended the Missouri River, then the Osage, to the villages of the Osage Indians in today's western Missouri. They were somewhere in Kansas when Pike learned that a Spanish force, "the most important ever carried on by the province of New Spain," was out to intercept his party. Sometime in October, Pike crossed the present border between Kansas and Colorado and camped along the Arkansas River near what would one day be the site of Bent's Fort.

On October 28, Pike sent Lieutenant James B. Wilkinson, the governor's son, and four companions down the Arkansas River with field notes and maps. He and the rest of the men headed west toward the Rocky Mountains. On November 15, Pike's party at last spied the Rockies, which reminded Pike of "a small blue cloud." As the men drew nearer, they saw the immensity and grandeur of the mountains in the Pueblo/Colorado Springs area, and on November 27 they climbed one of them, Cheyenne Peak. However, it remained for a later explorer to ascend Pikes Peak, named for the young lieutenant but not climbed by him or any member of his party.

Winter was approaching in earnest, and the poorly equipped expedition wandered in the southern Colorado Rockies for several weeks. By the early part of January, they had built a stockade near Pueblo to protect themselves from the elements. By February, Pike and most of the men had pushed farther south and had built another stockade near the headwaters of the Rio Grande. It was near there that the Spanish cavalry caught up with them.

After refusing the offer from the Spanish to take them to the Red River and let them go home, Pike and his little group were taken into custody and escorted first to Santa Fe and then to Chihuahua. Although all his papers, notes, and maps were confiscated by Spanish authorities, Pike was treated with the utmost courtesy by his captors. He had ample time to check out the military might of the Spanish army. In fact, so well did Pike do his homework that one eminent historian, William H. Goetzmann, has called his mission the most successful espionage operation in American history.

Finally, in the spring of 1807, Pike and his men were released from captivity and sent back to the United States. Pike reported from memory to an anxious General Wilkinson all that he had seen and heard in New Spain. Of course, nothing came of Wilkinson's and Burr's southwestern scheme, but as the War of 1812 approached, Pike's star continued to rise in the army as he was progressively promoted through the ranks. By March 1813, he was a brigadier general. The next month, at the Battle of York, Ontario, he was killed.

In addition to the military intelligence he brought back from New Spain, Pike was also responsible for the propagation of the "Great American Desert" myth, which discouraged American emigration across the Great Plains for years. He wrote that the vast, treeless prairie would restrict "our population to some certain limits..." and that "our citizens being so prone to rambling and extending themselves on the frontiers will, through necessity, be constrained to limit their extent on the west to the borders of the Missouri and Mississippi, while they leave the prairies incapable of cultivation to the wandering and uncivilized aborigines of the country."

CHAPTER FOUR

THE FIRST SETTLEMENT OF PUEBLO

·1822·

Major Jacob Fowler was a surveyor by profession. But it was not his vocation that brought him to the headwaters of the Arkansas River on a freezing day in January 1822. Rather, it was the craze for beaver hats among highbrow men and women in Europe and along America's eastern seaboard. Like so many men of adventure looking for instant fortunes, Fowler had taken up the life of a beaver trapper.

With a blustery wind driving relentlessly into his face, Fowler took time out from checking his traps that day to make the following brief entry in his journal:

> Sunday 6th Jany 1822 Went up to the Warm Spring Branch and Soot [set] two traps but the Weather is So Cold I beleve the bever Will not Come out—duglass [George Douglas, one of Fowler's trappers] in the Evening on driving up the Horses Reports Some Buffelow In Sight the Hunters Will look for them In the morning

This simple, scrawled paragraph denotes the appearance of Jacob Fowler on the site of the future city of Pueblo, Colorado.

Today Pueblo, nestled amid the majestic southern Rocky Mountains, is a thriving town of more than 100,000 people.

Although officially founded in 1858 and incorporated in 1870, the site of Pueblo was first permanently occupied by Fowler and his men during that cold January of 1822.

Four days before Fowler's diary entry, his partner in the trapping expedition, Colonel Hugh Glenn, had taken a few of their men and set out for Santa Fe. Several days before that, Spanish soldiers had confronted Fowler and Glenn and told them that Mexico had won its independence from Spain and that American trappers and traders were now welcome in Santa Fe and other New Mexican towns. Accordingly, "Conl glann and four men Set out...leaveing me With Eight men in an oppen Camp With the ballence of the goods after takeing Some things With Him to Sell So as to pay their Exspences."

Fowler and his men, fearing Indians, built a log house and horse pen and settled in to await Glenn's return.

On January 15, Fowler crossed the frozen Arkansas River "to look out a good Setuation for a new Settlement on the north Side of the River...." By now, Fowler assumed that Glenn was a captive of the Spanish in Santa Fe and that before long his own camp would be attacked by soldiers. Consequently, he decided to build a new house and horse pen on the far side of the Arkansas so that, if "the Spanierds appeer In a Hostill manner We Will fight them on the Ameraken ground, the River Hear being the line by the last tretey...."

The next day, Fowler and his men built a horse pen at the new site. On the 18th, the party built a new house that contained three rooms but only one outside door, "and that Close to the Hors Pen So that the Horses Cold not be taken out at night Without our knoledge." The next several days were spent hunting, trapping, and awaiting some word from Colonel Glenn.

Finally, in late January, news from Glenn arrived. He had been well received by the new Mexican authorities in Santa Fe after all and had "obtained premition to Hunt to trap and traid In the Spanish provences." Major Fowler and his small party made immediate plans to join Glenn in New Mexico.

Fowler's group left the Pueblo site on January 30, after spending close to a month in the area. The party traveled about ten miles west, and on the following day Fowler writes that he "struck the Spanish Road on our left Hand—which leads to touse [Taos, New Mexico] Which we followed and at five miles fell on a branch of the Crick on Which We lay last night."

Continuing southwestward, Fowler's expedition on February 6 crossed the imaginary line that separates today's states of Colorado and New Mexico. Two days later, they rendezvoused with Colonel Glenn in Taos. After trapping along the Rio Grande and among the Sangre de Cristo Mountains for several weeks, the reunited expedition started for the United States on June 1, arriving in St. Louis on July 15, 1822.

For years, the black mountain man, James P. Beckwourth, has been credited with establishing the first *permanent* settlement on the site of today's city of Pueblo. In his book, *The Life and Adventures of James P. Beckwourth*, the indomitable trapper and trader wrote:

> In the fall I returned to the Indian country, taking my wife with me. We reached the Arkansas about the first of October, 1842, where I erected a trading-post, and opened a successful business. In a very short time I was joined by from fifteen to twenty free trappers, with their families. We all united our labors, and constructed an adobe fort sixty yards square. By the following spring we had grown into quite a little settlement, and we gave it the name of Pueblo.

Actually, as can be seen in the excerpts from Jacob Fowler's journal—and depending of course on one's definition of permanent—Fowler may have beat Beckwourth to his claim by at least twenty years.

THE BUILDING OF BENT'S FORT
•1832•

When six-year-old Charles Bent, the eldest of Colorado's four noted Bent brothers, landed with his parents in St. Louis in 1806, he couldn't have known that he was destined to become one of the leading frontiersmen and traders of the southern Great Plains. A quarter of a century later, along with his younger brother, William, and a partner, Ceran St. Vrain, he would build a trading post on the north bank of the Arkansas River, near today's town of La Junta. Bent's small settlement would soon become the hub of a trading empire that covered hundreds of square miles of what is now Colorado, Wyoming, Utah, New Mexico, Arizona, Texas, Oklahoma, Kansas, and Nebraska.

When young Bent arrived in St. Louis, it was the jumping off place for the great American West. The young boy was fascinated by the rough-and-tumble frontiersmen he encountered along the waterfront. And although it had proceeded up the Missouri River from St. Louis two years earlier and had not been heard from for some time, the Lewis and Clark Expedition and its possible fate was still a primary subject of conversation among the merchants, hunters, and boatmen who thronged the wharves.

When Charles grew older, he joined the Missouri Fur Company and tried his hand at trapping beaver on the upper Missouri River. Because the company met with little success, Charles began looking for other ways to make his living, and he soon set his sights on the newly opened Santa Fe trade. Charles Bent pioneered the use of oxen to haul heavy freight wagons along the Santa Fe Trail, providing a financial respite to traders who could not afford higher-priced mules. In a letter written to the U. S. Secretary of War in October 1831, an associate noted that Bent's experiment with the oxen also "will answer the tripple [sic] purpose of, 1st, drawing the wagons; 2nd, the Indians will not steal them as they would horses and mules; 3rd, in case of necessity, part of the oxen will answer for provisions."

In the meantime, William Bent, some ten years younger than Charles, had successfully trapped along the upper reaches of the Arkansas River. When Charles and Ceran St. Vrain established their trading company in 1832, they asked William to come into the business with them.

William was placed in charge of the construction of the trading post on the Arkansas River. It was originally called Fort William in his honor. William was the on-site manager of Bent's Fort, allowing Charles and St. Vrain to travel to and from civilization with the merchandise required to outfit and supply the assemblage of American, Mexican, and French-Canadian trappers and traders who frequented the outpost.

Bent's Fort was a sight for sore eyes to weary travelers along the Santa Fe Trail. Matthew Field, the former actor, visited the post on his tour of the trail in 1839. He gave a vivid description of it in one of his articles in the New Orleans *Picayune*:

> Although built of the simple prairie soil, made to hold together by a rude mixture with straw and the plain grass itself, the strength and durability of the walls is surprising and extraordinary.... Round towers, pierced for cannon, command the sweep all around the building, the walls are not less than fifteen feet high, and the conveniences to launch destruction through and from above them are numerous as need be. Two hundred men might be garrisoned conveniently in the fort, and three or four hundred animals can be shut up in the corral. Then there are the store rooms, the extensive wagon houses, in which to keep the enormous, heavy wagons used twice a year to bring merchandise from the States, and to carry the skins of the buffalo and the beaver. Besides which the great wall encloses numerous separations—for domestic cattle, poultry, creatures of the prairie, caught and tamed, blacksmith and carpenter shops, &c. &c. Then the dwellings, the kitchens, the arrangements for comfort are all such as to strike the wanderer with the liveliest surprise, as though an "air built castle" had dropped to earth before him in the midst of the vast desert.

Another traveler, George Frederick Ruxton, an Englishman who frequented much of the Southwest during the Mexican War, visited Bent's Fort in 1847. Later, in his book *Life in the Far West*, he wrote that "the appearance of the fort is very striking, standing as it does hundreds of miles from any settlement, on the vast and lifeless prairie, surrounded by hordes of hostile Indians, and far out of reach of intercourse with civilized man...."

Bent's Fort reigned supreme on the Santa Fe Trail for several years. As time passed, however, and as the majority of wagon trains bypassed the outpost to travel the alternative Cimarron Cutoff, the "castle" in the desert lost its importance. William Bent, so the story goes, packed up his family and belongings one day in 1849 and rode out of the post, never to return. Some accounts even say that William, after failing to obtain a fair price for the fort from the U.S. Army, deliberately blew up the structure when he left it.

Today, Bent's Fort has been rebuilt in all its original glory, and it stands on the Colorado prairie near La Junta as a unit of the U.S. National Park Service. A visit there brings alive once again the sights and sounds of the Santa Fe Trail and the hardy merchants who frequented it.

CHAPTER SIX

A TREK ALONG THE SANTA FE TRAIL
· 1839 ·

When young Matthew C. Field appeared on the stage of the St. Louis Theatre that June evening in 1839, the house was packed. It was Field's last night as an actor, and he gave a stellar performance as Bristles in *The Farmer's Story*. After the play, Field offered a tear-provoking farewell speech to his audience and left the stage forever.

Twenty-eight-year-old Field was an Irish immigrant who had worked the theater circuit throughout the lower Mississippi River Valley for the past three years. Recently, he had developed respiratory problems, which were aggravated by a gastric ulcer. Although he was a good actor, he constantly feared that his theatrical career was only temporary and that one day he would no longer be accepted by the critics. Two young ladies' rejections of his marriage proposals compounded his maladies.

In July, Field and a small company of companions left Independence, Missouri, to travel over the Santa Fe Trail. They were bound for the legendary Mexican town that gave the trail its name. Field kept a diary of his journey, and when he returned to the United States, he wrote a lengthy series of articles based on his trip, entitled "Sketches of the Mountains and the Prairies." Newspapers were anxious to print firsthand accounts of the great American West, and Field quickly sold his series to the New Orleans *Picayune*, becoming an assistant editor of the paper as part of the deal.

The Santa Fe Trail was only eighteen years old when Field

used it to cross the southern plains in 1839. Meant to carry commercial traffic between Missouri and the newly independent country of Mexico, it was heavily used by American traders to haul merchandise to the isolated villages of New Mexico in exchange for furs, silver, and mules. Field's descriptions of places and events along the trail are among the most important and accurate in existence, and his observations provide keen insights into this far frontier of the late 1830s.

About his party's crossing from what is now Kansas into Colorado, near present-day Lamar, Field wrote:

> [U]pon the Arkansas, we reached an oasis to which we had long been looking forward. For weeks we had been revelling in anticipation upon the charms of this delightful place known to the old traders as Big Timber.... Here the expedition... released horses and mules from harness and turned them loose upon the rich grass.... A thick forest of venerable trees sheltered us from the heat, and beneath them wandered a stream yet cool with the mountain snow.... We saw the wild deer bounding from shore to shore and scarcely wetting a foot; and among the sunflower beds the huge back of a buffalo here and there was seen.... We were wearied down to the last gasp, and recklessly abandoning all ordinary precaution, we drank and bathed, and in the luxurious languor that followed we dropt beneath the trees and slept.

On August 18, when Field's party reached Bent's Fort— sometimes called Fort William after its builder, William Bent— they were refreshed from their recent sojourn at Big Timber. Here along the north bank of the Arkansas River, near today's town of La Junta, the Bent brothers and Ceran St. Vrain had built a magnificent adobe fort that served as a gathering place for fur trappers, traders, and various Indian tribes from all over the southern Great Plains. Field and his entourage were treated like royalty by the Bents and their employees.

To the hospitable courtesy of Robert Bent we were indebted for several days courteous and really delightful entertainment. The fatted calf was killed for us and the hoarded luxuries of Fort William were produced. The tenants of the fort were merry fellows, we were a set of youths well worthy to shake hands with them, and as such meetings, to the lonely sojourners in the desert, were indeed much like "angels' visits," the time was mutually appreciated....

Bent's Fort had only recently withstood an attack by Comanche Indians in which one of its defenders was killed and several valuable horses stolen. The Comanche raid was on everyone's tongue, and, of course, a breathtaking event such as this was not something Field would keep from his anxious New Orleans readership. In his spellbinding style, he later wrote:

The [Bent] brothers were at the time absent on one of the upper forks of the Platte, trading with the Pawnees, and the fort numbered only twenty tenants. It was just at sultry noon day, when the full flood of heat and light poured over the scene, the voice of the wind was mute, the insect ceased to hum, the wave of the Arkansas to murmur, and mid-day rivaled the night in hushed and breathless repose.... Suddenly the dozing inmates of the fort were startled by the war shriek of three hundred Camanches [sic], who appeared on the opposite bank of the Arkansas.... Almost in the same instant a faint cry reached the fort from the... guard, and before the alarmed tenants of the fortress had issued from the gate, all the animals were seen in full flight down to the green bank, over the Arkansas, and away, driven before some twenty red devils on wild horses, while the hapless Spaniard who had been on duty was seen to stagger towards the fort, and fall with three barbed arrows quivering in his body.

Eventually, Field arrived in Santa Fe, where he apparently enjoyed his stay thoroughly. He returned to St. Louis in the fall and went from there to New Orleans to take up his writing and editing assignments with the *Picayune*. Field later became the co-owner of a St. Louis newspaper. In the summer of 1844, he became ill again, and during early November, he boarded a vessel in Boston, bound for Mobile and New Orleans. Two days out of Boston, Field died and was quietly and unceremoniously buried at sea.

CHAPTER SEVEN

A HOLIDAY WITH FUR TRADERS
· 1839 ·

Twenty-two-year-old Elias Willard Smith could not have been happier. He had just graduated from Rensselaer Institute near Albany, New York, with a degree in engineering. As a reward for his four years of hard work, his father had presented him with a graduation present. And what a present it was! The elder Smith had given Elias the opportunity to accompany a group of fur trappers and traders to the Rocky Mountains and to live among them and the Indians for eleven months.

This was the opportunity of a lifetime for Smith. He had

heard about the famous mountain men who stalked the wilds of the Rockies and exposed themselves to the hostility of the Indians to trap beaver. Lately, with the demand for beaver diminished, some of them had joined the hide trade and concentrated on hunting the numerous buffalo that frequented the high plains. Now, for a brief period, Smith was going to be one of them.

Smith left Independence, Missouri, on August 6, 1839, in good company. With him were the venerable mountain men Andrew W. Sublette, Louis Vasquez, and Philip Thompson, the owner of Fort Davy Crockett, one of the destinations of the group. Also present was Baptiste Charbonneau, a noted guide and the son of Sacagawea, the Shoshone Indian woman who had accompanied Lewis and Clark to the Pacific.

The group followed the Santa Fe Trail across Kansas, and around September 1 they crossed into present-day Colorado along the Arkansas River east of Lamar. Smith's diary entry for September 2 reads:

> The prairie here is more rolling and sandy than we have seen it before. We had a view of the mountains this afternoon, but they are still one hundred and fifty miles distant. We are enabled to see this great distance on account of the clearness of the atmosphere. The atmosphere is very dry and clear—there being no dew at night. The weather is very warm. No fresh meat to-day. Buffalo is very scarce.

The expedition passed Bent's Fort the following day, and on September 5 the men sighted Pikes Peak, which had "snow on its summit at present." The next few days were uneventful, except for a meeting with a delegation of Arapaho Indians who came to camp one evening. Smith remembered the incident like this:

> They were all fine looking fellows, rather lighter-colored than our eastern Indians. Two or three squaws

accompanied them—also pretty good looking. The chiefs seated themselves around the fire, forming a ring with Mr. Vasquez and commenced smoking their long pipes, which they passed around several times.... Among their number was one Shian [Cheyenne] and one Blackfoot.

On September 13, Smith's entourage arrived at Fort Vasquez, just south of today's Platteville. The adobe fort was situated on the South Fork of the Platte River and was a gathering place for free trappers in the area. Smith was glad to visit a permanent settlement, and he slept that night under a roof for the first time in thirty-seven days.

Three days later, Smith and his companions headed west to Fort Davy Crockett, situated in the extreme northwest corner of Colorado at the confluence of the Vermillion and Green rivers. They crossed the Continental Divide on September 25 and arrived at Fort Davy Crockett on October 1.

On January 24, Smith and his party left the fort to return to Fort Vasquez. Winter at its worst caught them in the mountains, and at one point they had to eat their horses or starve. After several trials and tribulations with the weather, lack of food, and near exhaustion, the group sighted Fort Vasquez on April 24.

Unbeknown to Smith when he made his diary entry for April 26, he was about to embark on a river journey that had never before been attempted. The plan was to float seven hundred buffalo hides and four hundred buffalo tongues down the Platte River to the Missouri and from there to St. Louis. Smith wrote:

We started in a Mackinaw boat which had been made at the Fort at the foot of the mountains. This boat was thirty-six feet long and eight feet wide.... There were seven of us in company—sailing down the South Fork of the Platte to St. Louis. The water was very shallow and we proceeded with great difficulty, getting on sand bars every few minutes. We were obliged to wade and push the boat along most of the way for about three hundred miles, which took us forty-nine days.

Because game was scarce in the area, the men ate all the buffalo tongues by May 11. They traded whiskey with the Indians along the banks for meat before finally coming to a Pawnee village in June, where they partook of "the first vegetable food we had eaten in eleven months."

On June 22, Smith's boat passed the mouth of the Platte. The party was still more than one thousand miles from St. Louis. By the 24th, they had at last reached civilization, a small town in Missouri. Now, eager to end this voyage, the men sometimes forced themselves to travel eighty miles a day. Finally, on July 3, 1840, they arrived at St. Louis. They had come some two thousand miles in sixty-nine days.

In later life, Smith became a prominent engineer and participated in the design and construction of both the Detroit and the Chicago water works. He served in the Civil War as both quartermaster of the 113th Regiment of Infantry and major of the Seventh Regiment of Artillery, New York State Volunteers. After the war, Smith moved to Williamsburg, Virginia, and then to Georgetown, District of Columbia, where he lived until his death.

CHAPTER EIGHT

FRANCIS PARKMAN'S VISION
· 1846 ·

On the morning of August 17, 1846, a small party of men, southbound along the East Front of the Rocky Mountains, approached the site of present-day Colorado Springs. The leader of the group, Francis Parkman, who in a few years would be hailed as one of the greatest historians ever produced by the United States, wrote later that on the following day

> [b]efore sunrise in the morning the snow-covered mountains were beautifully tinged with a delicate rose-color. A noble spectacle awaited us as we moved forward. Six or eight miles on our right, Pike's Peak and his giant brethren rose out of the level prairie, as if springing from the bed of the ocean. From their summits down to the plain below they were involved in a mantle of clouds, in restless motion, as if urged by strong winds. For one instant some snowy peak, towering in awful solitude, would be disclosed to view. As the clouds broke along the mountain, we could see the dreary forests, the tremendous precipices, the white patches of snow, the gulfs and chasms as black as night, all revealed for an instant, and then disappearing from the view.

Parkman and his cousin, Quincy Adams Shaw, had left St. Louis on April 28 aboard the steamship *Radnor*, bound for

Westport Landing in western Missouri. The two young men had only recently graduated from Harvard College, and Parkman especially was keen on seeing the great American West before it became permanently spoiled by rapidly approaching "civilization." The trip was to be a "tour of curiosity and amusement to the Rocky Mountains," as Parkman phrased it, and as the warm days of May descended upon Westport, the pair headed across the prairie via the Oregon Trail.

Parkman's travels carried him to Fort Laramie, in today's state of Wyoming, where he spent considerable time. He was a keen observer, and even though his eyesight was greatly impaired and the mere task of writing was a hardship, he kept copious notes of all he saw and heard along the way. His notes, later painfully transcribed a few minutes at a time due to his failing eyesight, provided the basis for a series of successful articles that appeared in *Knickerbocker Magazine* in 1847 and later in his first book, *The Oregon Trail*, which appeared in 1849.

Although young and inexperienced with the ways and wonders of the West, Parkman and his cousin possessed, even then, a keen perception of what might one day happen to the pristine wilderness they were touring. Twenty-five years after *The Oregon Trail* appeared, Parkman wrote:

> I remember that, as we rode by the foot of Pike's Peak, when for a fortnight we met no face of man, my companion remarked, in a tone anything but complacent, that a time would come when those plains would be a grazing country, the buffalo give place to tame cattle, farmhouses be scattered along the water-courses, and wolves, bears, and Indians be numbered among the things that were. We condoled with each other on so melancholy a prospect....

Although Parkman and Shaw anticipated changes in the West, even they failed to foresee the dramatic impact those changes would have.

> We knew that there was more or less gold in the seams of those untrodden mountains; but we did not foresee that it would build cities in the waste and plant hotels and gambling-houses among the haunts of the grizzly bear.... We knew that more and more, year after year, the trains of emigrant wagons would creep in slow procession towards barbarous Oregon or wild and distant California; but we did not dream how Commerce and Gold would breed nations along the Pacific, the disenchanting screech of the locomotive break the spell of weird mysterious mountains, woman's rights invade the fastnesses of the Arapahoes.... We were no prophets to foresee all this; and, had we foreseen it, perhaps some perverse regrets might have tempered the ardor of our rejoicing.

In 1892, when Parkman wrote a preface for a new edition of *The Oregon Trail*, he continued to lament the passing of the great West. He wrote:

> Since that time [1872] change has grown to metamorphosis. For Indian teepees, with their trophies of bow, lance, shield, and dangling scalp-locks, we have towns and cities, resorts of health and pleasure seekers... Paris fashions, the magazines, the latest poem, and the last novel. The sons of civilization, drawn by the fascinations of a fresher and bolder life, thronged to the western wilds in multitudes which blighted the charm that had lured them. The buffalo is gone, and of all his millions nothing is left but bones. Tame cattle and fences of barbed wire have supplanted his vast herds

and boundless grazing grounds. Those discordant serenaders, the wolves that howled at evening about the traveller's camp-fire, have succumbed to arsenic and hushed their savage music. The wild Indian is turned into an ugly caricature of his conqueror; and that which made him romantic... is in large measure scourged out of him. The slow cavalcade of horsemen armed to the teeth has disappeared before parlor cars and the effeminate comforts of modern travel.... He who feared neither bear, Indian, nor devil, the all-daring and all-enduring trapper, belongs to the past or lives only in a few gray-bearded survivals. In his stead we have the cowboy, and even his star begins to wane. The Wild West is tamed, and its savage charms have withered.

As a young man, Parkman saw the American West at its pristine best. As yet unspoiled by farmers, miners, and the military, it was a region that few adjectives could justly describe. And the historian, whose fame by now was assured, sadly witnessed its closing as well. When Parkman died in 1893, the West was just another part of the giant that had become the United States of America.

CHAPTER NINE

KIT CARSON'S LONG MARCH

· 1848 ·

It was early June 1848, and Christopher ("Kit") Carson stood on the banks of the Grand River—today known as the Colorado— trying to figure out how to get across. The stream was swollen with melted snow, and Carson knew it could be quite dangerous.

Carson had left Los Angeles on May 4 on his way to Washington, D.C., where he was to deliver dispatches regarding the progress of the Mexican War in California. With him were a young army lieutenant, George Douglas Brewerton, and several companions. Carson's party had crossed southern California and the southern tip of today's Nevada and had headed northeastward across today's Utah until they entered what is now Colorado along the Grand, or Colorado, River.

So far, the long trip had been uneventful, but when Carson saw the rampaging river, he knew he had met his first major obstacle. Brewerton, who later wrote of his adventures with Carson, said

I remember celebrating my birthday... by standing upon the banks of the Grand River, and looking with a most rueful countenance and many secret forebodings upon the turbid current of the swollen stream.... [O]ne might suppose that a cold-bath in early summer was no great hardship; but in this case, I found that the association of the month with summer ended with its name; for the strong wind felt more like a December blast as it went rushing by, and the angry torrent at my feet, fed by the melting snows, was many degrees colder than the water of a mountain spring.

Carson and his men built a raft, cutting logs from the tall evergreen forest and lashing them together with the ropes they called *reatas*. When all was ready, Brewerton and several others jumped into the frigid waters and began to pull the raft across the rapidly moving river. Several minutes later and about one mile downstream, the raft came to rest against the same shore it had just left. Brewerton was struck by a log in midstream and had to be dragged to shore by his hair.

Back on dry land, Brewerton surveyed the dismal situation, and later he wrote:

Our situation was now far from pleasant, the only article of dress which we wore being our hats, the rest of our clothing having been left behind to come by another raft. To go up the rapids against the stream was out of the question; and to cross from where we were, with a considerable fall and jagged rocks just below us, equally impossible. So we had no recourse but to shoulder our baggage and travel back on foot, following, as nearly as the thickets would permit, the windings of the river....

Later that day, the men and their horses managed to get safely across the treacherous river. However, six rifles and several saddles were lost, in addition to all of Brewerton's notebooks, scientific samples, and sketches. Some of the crew even lost their clothes to the river and had to wrap themselves in what few blankets they had to protect themselves from the cold.

When Carson and his men left the Grand River, bound southward for Taos, New Mexico, they had only three days' provisions left. So they lived off the land, a chore made easier by Carson's years of experience as a mountain man, hunter, and guide. Finally, later in the month, they reached Carson's home in Taos. Proceeding immediately to Santa Fe, Carson met with Army authorities and then set out for the next destination on his long trip—Fort Leavenworth.

From Santa Fe, Carson went back through Taos, across the Colorado border to Pueblo, along the Eastern Front of the Rockies to Bijoux Creek, and down that stream to the South Fork of the Platte River. Following the Platte into what is now Nebraska, he cut cross-country to Fort Leavenworth. From there he went to Washington D.C., met with Army officials, and returned to New Mexico, arriving in October.

Kit Carson is one of America's genuine folk heroes. Born in backwoods Kentucky, he was apprenticed as a lad to a saddle maker in Missouri, from whom he eventually ran away. Carson later wrote of this time in his life that his master

was a good man, and I often recall the kind treatment I received at his hands. But taking into consideration that if I remained with him and served my apprenticeship, I would have to pass my life in labor that was distasteful to me, and being anxious to travel for the purpose of seeing different countries, I concluded to join the first party that started for the Rocky Mountains.

Carson became known far and wide as an expert scout, and he was hired by John C. Fremont to lead his exploration party through the Rocky Mountains and on to California. Later, the diminutive Carson—he was described by Lieutenant Brewerton as "rather below the medium height, with brown, curling hair, little or no beard, and a voice as soft and gentle as a woman's"— became a brevet brigadier general in the New Mexico Volunteers. For a while in late 1865 and early 1866, Carson served as commanding officer of Fort Union, New Mexico.

Next, Carson assumed command of Fort Garland, Colorado, a post he held until November 1867, when he retired from the Army. He and his family moved to Boggsville, Colorado, and in May 1868, at nearby Fort Lyon, the legendary Kit Carson died.

CHAPTER TEN

THE GREAT RAILROAD SURVEY

·1853·

As the 1850s got under way, national attention focused on the region that in a decade would become Colorado Territory. One of the most pressing issues facing the westward-looking American government was a proposed route for the transcontinental railroad. And the debate over where to put that rail line had torn the nation apart. The issue had become a political football. In the halls of Congress, politicians and lobbyists from North and South tried to out-talk and out-maneuver each other in order to get the railroad routed through their regions.

At the center of the controversy were two well-known men: Jefferson Davis, the U.S. secretary of war, and Thomas Hart Benton, a former Missouri senator. Several alternative routes from the Mississippi River to the Pacific Ocean had already been proposed, and naturally Davis, a Southerner, preferred one that traversed the southern sections of the country. Benton scoffed at the idea of running a railroad through the arid Southwest, saying the terrain was "so utterly desolate, desert, and God-forsaken that Kit Carson says a wolf could not make a living on it." Benton's own preference was a route that would roughly follow the thirty-eighth parallel from central Missouri to the Pacific.

There were many more proposals. In fact, there were so many—each promoted by its own regional advocates—that the question was debated for years before Congress came up with a scheme that it hoped would solve the dilemma.

Congress passed legislation on March 2, 1853, that gave Secretary of War Davis an imaginative but practically impossible mission. Davis was instructed to submit to Congress, within ten months, detailed reports, supported by actual field surveys, of *all* the proposed routes to the Pacific.

Davis quickly mobilized the Corps of Topographical Engineers and sent a series of surveying parties into the western wilderness to reconnoiter the several routes. In the meantime, Benton—not satisfied that the man Davis had hand-picked to survey the thirty-eighth parallel route, Captain John W. Gunnison, would report fairly—dispatched two other parties to render their own independent findings.

Gunnison was a West Point graduate who had entered the Army as an artilleryman and later transferred to the topographical engineers. He had assisted Howard Stansbury with his monumental survey of the Great Salt Lake region, and his experience in the mountains of Colorado and Utah made him a logical choice to head Davis's official survey expedition.

Gunnison and his party left Fort Leavenworth on June 23,

1853. Their mission was to survey a direct route that closely followed the thirty-eighth parallel through Kansas and into what would soon be Colorado Territory. The route generally followed the Arkansas River, passed Bent's Fort, and crossed the Continental Divide at Cochetopa Pass west of Pueblo. From the pass it snaked through the mountains, essentially following the river later named for Gunnison to its confluence with the Colorado River. Nearby, it crossed the border into what is now Utah.

Gunnison and his men made good progress until late October when they ran into a band of hostile Paiute Indians. At a spot northeast of Sevier Lake, Utah, the captain and seven of his comrades were killed by the warriors. The death of Gunnison left the survey party in a lurch, and work was suspended until the following year. In the meantime, Gunnison had already determined that the thirty-eighth parallel route was impractical due to the mixed terrain it crossed.

Despite the mammoth expense of multiple surveys, when all the reports were in (late as might have been expected), nobody paid any attention to them. Davis anticipated the government's final decision about where to put the rail line when, in 1858, he commented to Congress:

> [W]ith all due respect to my associates, I must say the location of this road will be a political question. It should be a question of engineering, a commercial question, a governmental question—not a question of partisan advantage or of sectional success in a struggle between parties and sections.

Although the surveys did not have much bearing on the eventual route of the first transcontinental railroad, they did uncover a vast amount of biological, geological, and ethnological data. In fact, this information about relatively unknown regions kept scientists and ethnographers busy for years to come.

Several place names in Colorado are reminders of the brave and scholarly Captain John W. Gunnison. The Gunnison River, a tributary of the Colorado; Black Canyon of the Gunnison National Monument; Gunnison National Forest, which covers nearly two million acres; and the town and county of Gunnison were all named in honor of the engineer.

CHAPTER ELEVEN

PIKES PEAK OR BUST
·1859·

It was a cold day in January 1859 when George Jackson trudged through the snow-clad Rocky Mountains about thirty miles west of the newly settled village of Denver. Jackson was a gold prospector with several years of experience as a California "Forty-niner." He had been digging for gold throughout the Central Rockies for a long time now, but to no avail. Jackson had only recently run out of supplies at his makeshift mining camp, but it was probably just as well. Of late, he had been giving serious consideration to leaving the prospecting business altogether and returning to Denver City to try to pursue a more normal life.

As he made his way toward Denver, Jackson came across some hot mineral springs on Clear Creek. There, he encountered a large herd of bighorn sheep and killed one for dinner. While he relaxed after eating, warmed by a spirited camp fire and flanked by his two devoted dogs, Jackson started thinking. What would he do in Denver? Prospecting was really the only life he knew. Maybe he should give it one more try. As he bedded down for the night, he made his decision. In the morning, he would dig around the hot springs to see if, just by chance, there might be some gold in what looked to be a promising area.

Early the next morning, Jackson began his search. All day, he walked up and down Clear Creek, carefully watching for any mineral flakes that might be exposed in the sand and gravel on the creek bottom. Finding a sizable sand bar, Jackson built a fire on it to thaw out its contents, hoping that the large bar might hold gold flakes that had washed downstream and become lodged within it.

Jackson had left his gold pan in his permanent camp, so he used his drinking cup as a substitute. As he swished the sand and water around the cup, slowly allowing the contents to fall back into the creek, sure enough, several flakes of gold sank to the bottom of the receptacle.

By the time darkness forced Jackson to quit, he had recovered about one ounce—ten dollars worth—of gold from the creek. Jackson covered all signs that the sand bar had been worked and returned to camp. He wrote in his diary that night:

After a good supper of meat—bread and coffee all gone—I went to bed and dreamed of riches galore in that bar. If I only had a pick and pan instead of a hunting knife and the cup, I could dig out a sack full of the yellow stuff. My mind ran upon it all night long.

I dreamed all sorts of things—about a fine house and good clothes, a carriage and horses, travel, what I would take to the folks down in old Missouri and everything you can think of—I had struck it rich! There were millions in it!

Over the next half century, the Clear Creek gold region yielded more than $100 million worth of the precious metal. Unfortunately, Jackson realized very little of this bonanza. After returning from Denver to the site of his claim in the spring of 1859, he panned for a while and then sold his interest to someone else for an unknown amount.

By the spring of 1859, driven by earlier reports of good gold diggings in the area, an estimated 100,000 prospectors and miners had begun the journey toward what is now Colorado, many with "Pikes Peak or Bust" scrawled across their wagons. Although most of the richest gold finds of that period were north of the famous mountain named for explorer Zebulon Pike, that didn't deter eastern travel-guide writers from lumping the entire region into one mysterious and gold-laden place called "Pikes Peak."

But most of the reports were exaggerated, and nearly half of the westward-bound miners never made it to Colorado. Some were killed by Indians in transit, and others who did reach their destinations faced poverty and starvation after they arrived. As many disheartened prospectors began the long trip back East, news of Jackson's find hit the tent camp at Denver City.

At about the same time that the "Pikes Peak" rush was on, silver was discovered near Virginia City in what is now Nevada. The combination of the two finds brought to the region literally thousands upon thousands of emigrants with riches in their eyes. Even played-out miners from California's 1849 gold-rush days crossed the mountains to take part in the scramble.

The prospect of wealth can ruin a man, and during the Pikes Peak gold rush, many men and their families did suffer financial and, in some cases, moral ruination. One observant miner rather succinctly described the wild and woolly times of the prospector when he wrote:

> It was a mad, furious race for wealth, in which many men lost their identity almost, and toiled and wrestled, and lived a fierce, riotous, wearing, fearfully excited life; forgetting home and kindred; abandoning old, steady habits; acquiring restlessness, craving for stimulant, unscrupulousness, hardihood, impulsive generosity, and lavish ways.

Other riches were to be discovered in the West in years to come, including silver at Leadville, Colorado, in 1877. But few of these finds would be as rich as the famous Pikes Peak gold rush of 1859, which, owing to the great influx of people, helped prepare the way for the region's entry into the United States as a territory in 1861.

CHAPTER TWELVE

THE CREATION OF THE DENVER MINT
· 1860 ·

Prospectors and miners who had rushed to the goldfields west of Denver City in the late 1850s were naturally elated at the news of rich finds in the area. Although many of them, after only a brief, disappointing stay in the mountains, headed for homes back East, a great number of the luckier ones actually struck it rich.

But even if a prospector was lucky enough to come upon a rich vein of gold or find a stream laden with the yellow dust, he still had a problem converting the metal to cash. While most merchants and saloon-keepers accepted gold dust as legal tender, the prospector usually came out on the short end of the stick when dealing with them. Since there was no standardization of the value of gold in the rough mining towns, the needy miner usually ended up swapping gold dust for food, drink, and merchandise worth only a fraction of the value of his metal.

Of course, there was an alternative, albeit a bad one. The miner could bring his gold to a shipping agent in Denver. It would then be sent back East to an assay office and properly weighed and valued. The gold would be purchased at the prevailing rate, and the payment would be sent back to the miner in the form of legal U.S. gold coins or check. When one considers the three months or more it took for this transaction to take place—plus the cost of shipping the gold to the assayer, the assayer's and broker's fees, and the insurance cost—it was sometimes simpler and just as cost-efficient to trade the raw gold for goods, even if one did get cheated now and then.

In the summer of 1859, three Eastern businessmen opened a gold brokerage office in Denver. Emanuel Gruber and brothers Austin and Milton Clark had already established a similar office at Leavenworth, Kansas, to accommodate gold-seekers working in the Colorado fields. As more and more gold was found in the mountains around Denver, it seemed a logical move to establish an office close to the source of the business.

Gruber and the Clarks were quick to see the problems the miners and prospectors faced with their abundance of gold but lack of ready cash. Accordingly, the threesome, operating as Clark, Gruber & Company, decided to open a private mint in Denver. The mint would buy the local miners' gold at the government-established price, refine the metal, and mint coins in various denominations that would be accepted anywhere as legal tender.

The mint opened in a red brick building at the corner of Market and Sixteenth streets. Assaying and minting equipment, along with dies, punches, and all the other necessary machinery, was purchased in Philadelphia. The company already had an abundant supply of raw gold since it had been brokering with the miners for several months.

After much preparation and publicity, Clark, Gruber & Company turned out its first gold coins on July 20, 1860. They were ten-dollar pieces. The company soon followed with twenty-dollar coins and, later still, with two and a half- and five-dollar pieces. Advertisements in local newspapers boasted of the company's unique services by stating:

> We have in connection with our Banking House, a MINT, and are prepared to exchange our Coin for Gold Dust. The native gold is coined as it is found, alloyed with silver. The weight will be greater, but the value the same as the United States coin of like denominations.

The editor of the *Rocky Mountain News* attended the grand opening of the mint. He was fascinated, as was most of the rest of the crowd, and he filed a glowing report of the proceedings:

> [W]e found preparations almost complete for the issue of the Pike's Peak coin. A hundred "blanks" had been prepared, weight and fineness tested and last manipulations gone through with, prior to their passage through the press. The little engine that drives the machinery was fired up, belts adjusted, and... the machinery was put in motion and "mint drops" of the value of $10 each began dropping into a tin pail with the most musical "chink." About a thousand dollars were turned out at the rate of fifteen or twenty coins a minute, which were deemed very satisfactory for the first experiment.
>
> The coins... are seventeen grains heavier than the U.S. coin of the same denomination.

On the face is a representation of the peak, its base surrounded by a forest of timber, and "Pike's Peak Gold" encircling the summit. Immediately under its base is the word "Denver," and beneath it "Ten D." On the reverse is the American Eagle encircled by the name of the firm, "Clark, Gruber & Co." and beneath the date, "1860."

In the first three months of operation, Gruber and the Clarks minted more than $120,000 worth of gold coins. Demand was so great that in December of the first year of operation, the company inaugurated a new service: the issue of paper currency that was exchangeable for the company's gold coins. Like the coins themselves, the paper money enjoyed considerable popularity.

In April 1862, the U.S. government decided to establish a mint in Denver and authorized purchase of the private Clark, Gruber & Company mint. The property changed hands in November. After manufacturing nearly $600,000 in gold coins in two and a half years, Clark, Gruber & Company got out of the minting business. But it stayed on in Denver as a bank that eventually merged into the First National Bank.

Gruber and the Clark brothers were visionaries, but even in their wildest dreams they could never have guessed how valuable a single coin from their Denver mint would one day be. Although popular and commonly circulated in its time, a Clark, Gruber & Company gold coin is so rare today that one in excellent condition can bring as much as sixteen thousand dollars among collectors.

CHAPTER THIRTEEN

THE SAND CREEK MASSACRE
·1864·

Chief Black Kettle was proud of his American flag, given to him in 1860 by Indian Commissioner A. B. Greenwood. Over the years, it had become a symbol of his promise to live peaceably at his camp on Sand Creek, a tributary of the Arkansas River in southeastern Colorado. He and his band of Cheyennes, along with the few Arapahoes who shared the encampment, hoped to live in harmony with the white man.

Colonel John M. Chivington had other ideas. Chivington, a Methodist-Episcopal minister by profession, had answered the call to join the Colorado militia at a time when feelings were running high against the Indians. The colonel considered it his obligation to annihilate "women- and children-killing savages" at every chance he got. On one occasion he exclaimed, "Damn any man who is in sympathy with Indians."

One can only speculate why some white men lived their entire lives in bitter hatred of the Indians. It is true there were many men whose family and friends had been exterminated by one tribe or another in those days when both races were at each other's throats for real or supposed wrongs. Chivington, however, stands above most of the rest as a genuine Indian-hater, and his role in history, especially by today's standards, is disgusting.

Chivington was born in Ohio in 1821. He served as a minister in his native state, as well as in Illinois, Missouri, Kansas, and Nebraska, before moving to Colorado in 1860. There, he actively preached in the gold-mining camps, and he is generally credited with organizing the first Methodist Sunday School in Denver.

When the Civil War broke out, Chivington was offered a commission as chaplain in the First Regiment of Colorado Volunteers, but he refused the "praying" position in favor of a "fighting" one. When the First Regiment was sent to New Mexico a short time later, the Fighting Parson, as he was called, demonstrated his prowess in combat. He was instrumental in driving the Confederates from the Southwest at the Battle of Glorieta Pass.

As the Civil War intensified and increasing numbers of regular army troops were called to duty back East, some of the Indian tribes took the opportunity to attack unprotected white settlements along the frontier. Several areas were hit hard by marauding bands of Southern Cheyennes and Arapahoes. When local authorities decided to take the war to the Indians, the Fighting Parson, known for his hatred of Indians, was the logical choice to lead the troops.

Black Kettle had been instructed by Major Edward Wynkoop at Fort Lyon, Colorado Territory, to fly his American flag high above his tipi as a sign of his friendship toward whites. Wynkoop assured the old chief that white soldiers would not harm him. But Colonel Chivington, when advised of Black Kettle's situation, replied that all was fair when it came to defeating Indians. He rode off to his destiny vowing that he would take no prisoners.

On the morning of November 29, 1864, Chivington's Third Colorado Volunteers fell upon the five hundred sleeping Indians in Black Kettle's camp with instructions from their commander to "kill and scalp all, big and little, nits make lice!" Hundreds of unarmed Indians ran out of their tipis, alarmed at the sight of so many approaching soldiers but still under the impression that the Army would protect them. When troopers dropped one Cheyenne after another with their carbines, it became all too clear what was going on.

When the fighting was finally over—if it can be called fighting, since the Indians had very little chance to arm and defend themselves—Chivington's volunteers had killed between two hundred and four hundred Cheyennes and Arapahoes. The vast majority of the dead were women and children. Any wandering survivors were sought out and summarily killed. The soldiers spent the rest of the day scalping and mutilating the bodies of their victims.

Chivington returned to Denver a conquering hero and even displayed the bloody scalps and body parts of the vanquished in a local theater. But there were those who condemned his actions, and the Fighting Parson's escapade finally became the subject of a congressional investigation. After hearing seven hundred pages of testimony, the committee ordered the colonel's court-martial. However, it also allowed him to resign his commission and thereby escape punishment for his atrocious deed.

Black Kettle's wife, shot nine times by the soldiers, somehow lived and escaped the massacre with her husband, who miraculously was unhurt. In the ensuing months, even after his betrayal by the Army, the Cheyenne chief continued to try to convince his own and neighboring tribes that peace was better than war. The old man's reward came almost exactly four years to the day after the Sand Creek affair. On a cold November day in 1868, he, his wife, and 103 other peace-seeking Cheyennes and Arapahoes were massacred on the Washita River in Indian Territory by Lieutenant Colonel George Armstrong Custer.

What became of Chivington after his reprehensible attack on Black Kettle's peaceful camp? He engaged in the freighting business in Nebraska for a while, then went to California, back to Ohio, and finally to Denver again. He died of cancer in 1894, still trying to explain his actions on that fateful November day thirty years earlier.

CHAPTER FOURTEEN

THE BLAZING OF THE GOODNIGHT-LOVING TRAIL
·1866·

In 1869, Charles Goodnight made an important decision. A Texas rancher and trail-driver, he was already widely known among cattlemen as the partner of Oliver Loving, one of the first men to bring Texas longhorns into Colorado Territory. But Loving had died the previous year, and now Goodnight decided to leave Texas and try his hand at organizing a ranch in southern Colorado.

As he stood on the banks of the Arkansas River, west of Pueblo, he was amazed at the absolute beauty of the spot. Here, among canyons lined with cottonwoods and box-elders, he would build a herd the likes of which Colorado had never seen before. The range, watered by the melted snows of the nearby Rocky Mountains, was lush, and Goodnight's business sense told him that the thousands of cattle he would raise here would yield rich rewards when the railroad got as far as Denver.

Goodnight was just the man to build such a ranch. He had been born the day before the Alamo fell in March 1836, in far-off Illinois. He moved to Texas as a lad and helped out on the poor farm that his stepfather had left Illinois to obtain. Upon reaching adulthood, Goodnight became a scout and independent ranger, but at the same time, he continued learning about the vast herds of Texas longhorn cattle that seemed to be everywhere.

During the Civil War, Goodnight served the Confederacy in Texas as a ranger keeping peace with the Comanches along the frontier. When the war was over, hundreds of Texas farmers and ranchers put down their weapons and returned home to find their spreads ruined by neglect. And they found that the longhorns, in the absence of care, had multiplied manyfold and were overgrazing much of the sparse range. Clearly someone needed to devise a way to market the cattle.

Even before a man named Joseph McCoy dreamed of driving Texas cattle northeastward to the newly founded railhead town of Abilene, Kansas, Goodnight and Loving were playing with the idea of driving a herd westward into New Mexico, then northward to Denver, Colorado Territory. In 1866, the two men got a sizable herd together and started west toward the Pecos River. They crossed the stream and proceeded to Fort Sumner, New Mexico Territory. After selling some of the cattle there, Goodnight returned to Texas to round up a new herd, while Loving continued on to Denver. There, he sold the rest of the herd to John W. Iliff. The trail the two partners had carved from Fort Belknap, Texas, to Denver became known as the Goodnight-Loving Trail.

The following year, Loving was severely wounded by Comanche Indians as the partners moved another herd along their trail. He died at Fort Sumner, but Goodnight went on and delivered the cattle to their buyers. On his way back through Fort Sumner, he had his partner's body exhumed and laid in a crudely made metal coffin. Goodnight placed the coffin in a wagon and drove it back to Texas for a proper burial, thus fulfilling his friend's deathbed wish.

After Goodnight returned to Colorado in 1869 to establish his ranch along the Arkansas River, success came rapidly. He now felt secure enough to take a wife, and the following year he went back East to marry his Tennessee-born sweetheart, Mary Ann Dyer. He brought his new bride back to Colorado, where he expected they would spend the rest of their lives together.

Goodnight became active in the community of Pueblo. He was an organizer of the town's first bank, the Stock Growers Bank of Pueblo. The future seemed bright for Goodnight and his fellow ranchers in southern Colorado, but in reality the nation was on the brink of one of the worst depressions ever to hit North America—the Panic of 1873. Goodnight and his neighbors hit rock bottom, and Goodnight later lamented that "the panic wiped me off the face of the earth."

By 1876, Goodnight's good life in Colorado was over. He took his wife and what few cattle he still owned and went back to Texas. There, in the Palo Duro Canyon, Goodnight established a new ranch. Over the next few years, he was instrumental in developing and breeding new strains of domestic cattle. With an Irish immigrant named John Adair, he helped amass almost one million acres, which supported nearly 100,000 cattle. The JA Ranch rapidly became one of the largest and most famous spreads in all of North America.

After Adair died, Goodnight decided to slow down and divided the JA with Mrs. Adair. "I am heartily sick of men and ranches," he wrote her. But he still maintained more than 100,000 acres upon which he raised cattle and some buffalo. Goodnight and his wife were the founders, in 1898, of Goodnight College, as well as the organizers of two churches in West Texas. Mary Ann Goodnight died in 1926, and Charles followed in 1929.

Texas lays claim to Charles Goodnight, and with his fame as part owner of the magnificent JA Ranch, maybe rightly so. But before he was a rancher in Texas, he was a Coloradan, and he and his spread near Pueblo were known far and wide. As his noted biographer, J. Evetts Haley, once put it, Goodnight's "force, his fearlessness, his plains-craft, and his mental vigor... will be remembered throughout the West as long as the story of cattle and horses intrigues the fancy of men."

CHAPTER FIFTEEN

J.W. POWELL'S ROCKY MOUNTAIN EXPEDITION
· 1868 ·

On July 8, 1868, Major John Wesley Powell, a bearded, one-armed veteran of the Civil War, left Cheyenne, in what is now Wyoming, and headed south along the Front Range of the Rocky Mountains toward Denver. With Powell was a small group of people whom Powell's biographer, Wallace Stegner, described as "too late in time to be called explorers, too unskilled to deserve the name of frontiersmen." The party was fancifully called "The Rocky Mountain Scientific Exploring Expedition," and its mission was basically stated in its name.

Although Powell's crew was largely made up of amateurs interested in natural and geographical exploration rather than those trained in the discipline, the party made its way to Denver without incident. Among the group were two women, Major Powell's wife, Emma Dean Powell, and his sister, Nellie Powell Thompson, as well as Nellie's husband, Almon Thompson. The guide, a veteran mountain man named Jack Sumner, described the party as "about as fit for roughing it as Hades is for a Powder house."

In any event, Powell, not a professional explorer yet himself, was satisfied with the group, and he planned to make the best of it among the wildlands of Colorado that summer. After all, he did have the support of several scientific institutions back East, and he did not intend to fall into disfavor with them in case bigger and better exploration opportunities might arise.

One of Powell's pressing desires was for his party to ascend Long's Peak, a feat never before accomplished by white men. The major assembled a climbing party consisting of himself, his brother Walter Powell, and several others, including the guide, Sumner. After a grueling climb through rough timber and sheer rock cliffs and slides, the party finally arrived at the crest of the peak. One of the members wrote later:

> After a pretty hard climb we did it, built a monument on the top, raised a flag, threw some wine on the monument & the little that remained in the bottle was drank by 5 of the party, 2 of us withstanding all entreaties did not drink on Longs peak, whatever the papers may say to the contrary.

The amateur scientists scurried back and forth along the top of Long's Peak like children in a playground. The view was breathtaking, and although the plant growth at this altitude and temperature was sparse, the sharp-eyed members managed to find many specimens. A botany expert with the group wrote:

> Nothing but Granite on the top afforded a poor foothold for Botanists yet some pretty mosses grew in the shadows of some large rocks, or close to the edges of the patches of snow... a few Lichens, i.e., only a few kinds, but many of a species grew and flourished on the otherwise bare sides of the Granite rocks.... No flowers here too high for them.... A few species of flies gnats &c. Several species of Beetles: and many thousands of a peculiar Grasshopper were all the living things I found. No, not all a very pretty white Butterfly... passed over the top which contains 5 or 6 acres... caused me quite a chase....

From Long's Peak, Major Powell's expedition marched westward to Hot Sulphur Springs, arriving in August. There, the party met Schuyler Colfax, speaker of the U.S. House of Representatives; Alexander C. Hunt, governor of Colorado Territory; and the famous journalist Samuel Bowles. Bowles was particularly interested in Powell's project and gave him considerable press. However, the major also confided in the newspaperman his plans for an even greater undertaking, and Bowles gave his vast readership a preview of events to come when he wrote:

> From here the explorers will follow down the Grand River, out of [Estes] Park into western Colorado, and then strike across to the other and larger branch of the great Colorado River, the Green, and upon that or some of its branches, near the line of Utah, spend the winter in camp... preparing for the next summer's campaign. The great and final object... is to explore the upper Colorado River and solve the mysteries of its three hundred mile canyon. They will probably undertake this next season by boats and rafts from their winter camp on the Green.

And that is exactly what Powell did. On May 24, 1869, the major wrote:

> The good people of Green River City turn out to see us start. We raise our little flag, push the boats from shore, and the swift current carries us down. Our boats are four in number.... We take with us rations deemed sufficient to last ten months....

And so Powell and his newly outfitted expedition of 1869 rode down the Colorado River and into the pages of history as the first men to float successfully through the Grand Canyon.

CHAPTER SIXTEEN

THE BATTLE OF BEECHER ISLAND
·1868·

Roman Nose was a troubled man. As he sat in camp listening to distant gunfire, he debated whether to ride off immediately to the fight with the white men or wait awhile longer, until the magic medicine that had protected him in battle so many times before could be restored. Watching row after row of his tired, dejected Cheyenne brothers stream up the hill from the river several miles away was agonizing for the great war leader, for he knew from the sound of the battle that his warriors, some of them armed only with bows and arrows, were under great duress from the repeating firearms of the white men.

Roman Nose had lost his medicine when he unknowingly ate some food that had been touched by an iron fork. Now, he was not only agitated about that loss, but he was puzzled about the way the battle below was unfolding. How could fifty white civilian scouts and plainsmen—even though experienced in Indian warfare and described once by General Philip Sheridan as "first-class, hardy frontiersmen,"—hold off a combined war party of nearly seven hundred Cheyenne, Sioux, and Arapaho warriors?

Major George A. Forsyth had recruited his men from the hodge-podge of civilians who traditionally hung around the Army posts scattered across the prairie. Considering he could pay each man only fifty dollars a month—seventy-five if he could provide his own horse—Forsyth thought he had done a pretty fair job of assembling a crack fighting unit to track down rowdy Indians during the late summer of 1868. For his second in command,

Forsyth had chosen Lieutenant Frederick H. Beecher, a nephew of the famed abolitionist preacher, Henry Ward Beecher.

The unit left Fort Hays, Kansas, on August 29, 1868. On September 16, Forsyth and his command pitched camp on the west bank of the Arikara Fork of the Republican River in northeastern Colorado. The following morning, as Forsyth was inspecting his men and their equipment, a large party of Indians swept down upon them. Quickly shouting commands amidst the confusion, the major ordered his troops to retreat to a small island where they could dig into the sandy beach. The river was nearly dry, so the fifty-one men, leading their horses and carrying all the supplies they could, crossed the channel in record time.

The men were armed with Spencer seven-shot repeating carbines and Colt percussion, six-shot revolvers. Every man had 170 rounds of ammunition. Another four thousand rounds were held in reserve. Although the rapid fire produced by the frontiersmen's state-of-the-art weapons momentarily surprised the charging Indians, they swept down on the island again and again. In one onslaught, Major Forsyth was wounded twice. A few minutes later, a third round struck him in the skull as he uttered, "We are beyond all human aid, and if God does not help us there is none for us."

Meanwhile, back at the Cheyenne encampment, Roman Nose could wait no longer. Chided by some of the braves for remaining in camp while his fellow warriors were being slaughtered, the Indian armed himself, jumped on his horse, and sped across the prairie to battle. Upon arrival, Roman Nose organized a charge. As he drew nearer to the white men's defenses, one of them fired his rifle and hit the brave Cheyenne in the small of the back. Roman Nose fell from his horse, mortally wounded. Soon after his friends carried him away, Roman Nose died.

By nightfall, Forsyth, who had not succumbed to his three gunshot wounds, counted twenty-four men dead or wounded, including Lieutenant Beecher. Nearly half his force was disabled! Fortunately for the major and his men, the Indians did not attack the next day. Forsyth took advantage of the lull to send two messengers about one hundred miles to Fort Wallace with requests for relief.

On the fourth day of battle, the frontiersmen's rations gave out, and they were reduced to eating the rotting flesh of their long-dead horses. The Indians, unwilling to risk any more manpower on whites who were starving to death anyway, waited for hunger to take its toll. Forsyth dispatched two more messengers in case the first pair had failed to get through. The wait was agonizing, and the stranded men's hunger and thirst became almost unbearable.

But the first two messengers had made it safely to Fort Wallace, and the commander there, Lieutenant Colonel Henry C. Bankhead, immediately sent a message to Captain Louis H. Carpenter, who was in the field with his all-black company of the Tenth Cavalry. When Carpenter and his unit approached the island on the eighth day of the siege, the Indians broke camp and retreated. Colonel Bankhead and more soldiers from Fort Wallace arrived the following day.

Major Forsyth spent two full years recuperating from his wounds. Nothing was accomplished by the battle, except that General Sheridan called off the formation of any more such "civilian-soldier" units to fight Indians on their own turf.

Out of respect for the young lieutenant killed early in the battle, the island in the middle of the river was named Beecher Island, and the conflict there was known among whites thereafter as the Battle of Beecher Island. The Indians, however, honored their own brave warrior. For years afterwards, they called the skirmish the "Fight Where Roman Nose Was Killed."

CHAPTER SEVENTEEN

THE GREAT DIAMOND HOAX
·1872·

Heads turned and tongues wagged as the two disheveled prospectors made their way down Powell Street in San Francisco that summer day in 1872. After all, the city was well on its way to becoming the metropolis of the Pacific Coast. One would have thought that all that nasty prospecting for gold and groveling around in the dirt for silver was over. California was civilized, and the days of the Gold Rush were long gone.

But unbeknown to the pedestrians along Powell Street, these dirty, ill-clad men were neither gold nor silver prospectors. They had something in their sack that had never been found in North America before. And when the news of what they had brought with them from Colorado spread throughout the financial district of San Francisco, a near-riot broke out.

It may have shocked the erudite San Franciscans, but it probably would have come as no surprise to the mountaineers of Colorado that diamonds, yes diamonds, had recently been discovered in their own backyard. After all, had not their territory yielded some of the most fantastic gold finds of the century, starting with the Pikes Peak gold rush that attracted more than fifty thousand prospectors by 1859? And was not silver, gold's sister metal, being extracted right this instant from the Rocky Mountains in unprecedented amounts?

The Colorado diamond craze all started that day in 1872, when the two men, Philip Arnold and John Slack, both originally from Kentucky, arrived in San Francisco and made their way to the bank at the far end of Powell Street. The two had never seen such a fancy bank before, and they spent a few moments looking about the place, while equally curious stares were directed at them.

The men finally walked up to a vacant window and pushed a heavy, dirty sack toward the wide-eyed teller. They told the man they wanted to leave the sack for safekeeping while they had a look around town. The teller called his manager, who explained that he needed to see the contents of the sack before he could take responsibility for it.

One of the old prospectors untied the leather strings that held the mouth of the sack closed. Carefully picking up the bag by the bottom, he poured its contents onto the counter. Out rolled hundreds of uncut diamonds, ranging in size from no bigger than a match head to the size of a twenty-dollar gold piece!

After a few minutes of conversation, the prospectors raked the diamonds back into the sack and again pushed the bag toward the teller, who this time cheerfully issued a claim ticket. All eyes were upon the men as they casually left the building and walked down Powell Street to see the sights of San Francisco.

It did not take long for news of the diamonds to spread like wildfire throughout the bank. Within days, everyone in San Francisco's financial community had heard the story of the two grizzled old men who had mysteriously appeared in the Bank of California with a large portion of diamonds.

Curiosity fired by greed immediately developed among the bank's officers over the origin of what appeared to be very fine diamonds. Thinking the prospectors naive and simplistic, the bankers decided they would attempt to learn the location of the diamond fields.

They approached the two prospectors, and after much talk and pleading, the pair were "persuaded" to reveal the location of their diamond mine on the premise that the bankers were interested in investing in the venture. A representative of the bank was immediately dispatched to Colorado to conduct a firsthand inspection of the diamond fields. The prospectors blindfolded him when they drew near the site, which turned out to be four days from Black Buttes, Wyoming, on a mesa in northwestern Colorado. Permitted to hunt to his heart's content, the representative was quick to find much more evidence, including rubies, that pointed to the great value of the diamond fields.

Meanwhile, back in California, after hearing the glowing report of their field representative, the bankers decided to ask Tiffany's of New York to verify the quality of the stones. The esteemed jewelry firm reported that if the diamonds were available in quantity, they would be worth a "rajah's ransom."

Within a short time of receiving all this good news, a syndicate of Californians promptly invested ten million dollars and organized the San Francisco and New York Mining and Commercial Company. The two prospectors "grudgingly" allowed themselves to be bought out for $600,000. After Henry Janin, a well-known mining engineer, personally inspected the diamond site and testified to its authenticity, the syndicate was barraged with requests from others trying to get in on the action. Before the mad rush was over, more than twenty-five companies had been organized, offering more than $200 million worth of stock. All had charters to exploit the diamond fields of Colorado.

Some time later, Clarence King, who later became the first director of the U.S. Geological Survey and who only recently had mapped the region where the diamonds were supposedly found, reported that the site had been "salted." No diamonds naturally existed there. Furthermore, a detailed investigation of the two prospectors' diamonds showed they had cutters' marks on them. Finally, a report from London revealed that the Kentucky men had purchased a quantity of inferior stones there the previous year.

Arnold and Slack had completely duped the California financiers! Millions of dollars were lost, and not one diamond was ever found! Lawsuits were filed, but what could be done? The investors had taken part in the endeavor only after they had investigated it and thought it to be perfectly legitimate.

Nobody was left smiling after the hoax was exposed except Arnold and Slack. Arnold did find it in his heart to settle partially with the hoodwinked investors out of his proceeds from the scam. But he still had enough money left to live comfortably in Kentucky until his death in 1878. The other con man retired to New Mexico, where he became a coffin-maker.

CHAPTER EIGHTEEN

A RAMBLE IN THE ROCKIES
• 1873 •

Few pairs in history were more unlikely than the man and woman who found themselves climbing to the top of Long's Peak on a freezing autumn day in 1873. She was Isabella Bird, a British spinster and daughter of an Anglican churchman; he was "Mountain Jim" Nugent, a one-eyed, hard-drinking Irishman who could quote the classics as well as he could hunt, scout, and get into trouble.

Isabella had recently come to the United States from the Hawaiian Islands. Both places were planned destinations on an eighteen-month, around-the-world tour. From California, Isabella had traveled to Cheyenne, Wyoming, and then south into Colorado, establishing a sort of home base at Estes Park. She discovered Mountain Jim's cabin soon after reaching the park and wrote later that the

owner came out, a broad, thickset man, about the middle height, with an old cap on his head, and wearing a grey hunting suit much the worse for wear (almost falling to pieces, in fact), a digger's scarf knotted around his waist, a knife in his belt, and "a bosom friend," a revolver, sticking out of the breast pocket of his coat; his feet, which were very small, were bare, except for some dilapidated moccasins made of horse hide.... His face was remarkable. He is a man about forty-five, and must have been strikingly handsome. He has large grey-blue eyes, deeply set, with well-marked eyebrows, a handsome aquiline nose, and a very handsome mouth. His face was smooth shaven except for a dense mustache and imperial.... One eye was entirely gone, and the loss made one side of the face repulsive, while the other might have been modeled in marble. "Desperado" was written in large letters all over him.

Forty-two-year-old Isabella was quite impressed by Mountain Jim, and the pair became the best of friends. When she expressed a desire to climb Long's Peak, her neighbors tried to discourage her, saying it was too late in the year. But Mountain Jim came swaggering in one day and announced that he would be happy to guide her up the steep slopes of the nearly fifteen-thousand-foot peak, which had been climbed for the first time only five years earlier.

When all was ready, Isabella, Mountain Jim, and two young companions left the warmth and safety of Estes Park and began the one-day journey to Long's Peak. They pitched camp that evening at the base of the mountain in twenty-degree weather. Mountain Jim made sure the night's accommodations were as comfortable as possible for his British companion. Later, Isabella wrote:

> [T]hough his manner was certainly bolder and freer than that of gentlemen generally, no imaginary fault could be found. He was very agreeable as a man of culture as well as a child of nature; the desperado was altogether out of sight. He was very courteous and even kind to me.... That night I made the acquaintance of his dog "Ring," said to be the best hunting dog in Colorado.... In a tone as if speaking to a human being, his master, pointing to me, said, "Ring, go to that lady, and don't leave her again to-night...." Ring lay at my back to keep me warm.

Early the next morning, the small party assaulted Long's Peak. The going was slow. Jim tied a length of rope between himself and Isabella, in case she slipped on the loose rock along the steep slopes. The air was rarefied, and as the two breathlessly struggled higher and higher, there were times, Isabella reported later, that Jim actually "dragged me up." Still, these two persisted. On the final leg of the ascent, Isabella looked down and wrote later that, "one slip, and a breathing, thinking human being would lie 3,000 feet below, a shapeless, bloody heap!"

At one especially precipitous place near the top, the climbers took one full hour to travel five hundred feet. They finally conquered the mountain, and though she was thoroughly exhausted, battered, and bruised, Isabella could still comment:

> From the summit were seen in unrivalled combination all the views which had rejoiced our eyes during the ascent. It was something at last to stand upon the storm-rent crown of this lonely sentinel of the Rocky Range, on one of the mightiest of the vertebrae of the backbone of the North American continent, and to see the waters start for both oceans.

Isabella spent about four months in America. She published accounts of her experiences in the English weekly *Leisure Hour* in 1878. The stories, which were written in the form of letters to her sister, were published in book form in 1879, under the title, *A Lady's Life in the Rocky Mountains.*

Isabella continued her globetrotting after leaving the United States. For thirty more years, she traveled extensively, finding time along the way to help organize five hospitals and a college for medical missionaries in the Far East and India. In 1904, after a lifetime of adventure and selfless humanitarian pursuits, Isabella died as a result of a long illness.

As for Mountain Jim, Isabella had tried in vain to reform him and get him to give up drinking. "As I looked at him, I felt a pity such as I never before felt for a human being," she wrote in one of her letters. But the kindly Irishman had always replied, "Too late! Too late! for such a change...." And too late it was. Just a few months after leaving Colorado, Isabella was saddened to learn that Jim had been killed in a gunfight.

CHAPTER NINETEEN

THE CANNIBALISM OF ALFRED PACKER
· 1874 ·

Alfred Packer was as cold as he had ever been in his life. As he groped his way through the deep snow of the Colorado Rockies, searching for the temporary camp where he had left his five companions earlier in the day, he must have questioned his decision to make this late-winter trip.

Alfred (traditionally spelled "Alferd") Packer had been born in Pennsylvania. He served a short stint in the Union Army during the Civil War and was discharged due to "disability." Then he became a shoemaker and migrated westward with the thousands of other shopkeepers and farmers who believed they would find fabulous riches at the end of their long, arduous journeys. But no fortune awaited Packer, who bummed around the mining camps and prospected here and there.

In November 1873, Packer and twenty-one other men left Bingham Canyon, Utah, and headed east toward Colorado. By mid-January, the group had arrived at the winter camp of the Ute chief Ouray, which was on the Gunnison River near Montrose. The amiable chief attempted to persuade Packer and his companions to stay with him and his people, warning of the intense snowstorms that regularly visited the mountains during the winter. But after a few days in camp, Packer and five other men decided they would continue their journey to the rich gold fields of central Colorado. The men said goodbye to Ouray and their companions on February 9.

Now, here was Packer, about ten days from Ouray's camp,

as best as he could recollect, and already out of food. He had left his companions earlier in the day to try to find some source of nourishment other than the pine gum and plant buds they had been eating since their food ran out. For some reason, the party had left Ouray's village with only seven days' worth of food for one man. It did not take long for six men to go through the short supply, and by the fourth day out, only one pint of flour was left. Food had been extremely scarce for nearly a week now.

When Packer entered his own encampment at the end of a fruitless day searching through the deep snow for food, he found one of his companions

> sitting near the fire roasting a piece of meat which he had cut out of the leg of the German butcher. The latter's body was lying the furthest off from the fire down the stream, his scull [sic] was crushed in with the hatchet. The other three men were lying near the fire, they were cut in the forehead with the hatchet some had two some three cuts—I came within a rod of the fire, when the man saw me, he got up with his hatchet toward me when I shot him sideways through the belly, he fell on his face, the hatchet fell forward. I grabbed it and hit him in the top of the head.

Finding himself suddenly alone, Packer built a crude lean-to, covered it with pine boughs, covered the bodies of the dead men, and "fetched to the camp the piece of meat that was near the fire. I made a new fire near my camp and cooked the piece of meat and ate it."

Every day afterwards, Packer attempted to escape his winter prison, "but could not so I lived off the flesh of these men the bigger part of the 60 days I was out." Finally, the snow melted, and Packer came out of the mountains, arriving at the Los Pinos Agency on April 16. He survived his trek out of the freezing wilderness by eating the flesh of his companions, some of which he had carried with him.

Curious authorities at Los Pinos questioned Packer about his five fellow travelers. In time, he admitted eating their bodies and escorted a search party to the site of their camp. What remained of the five bodies was buried, and Packer was arrested and jailed at nearby Saguache. He escaped before he could be tried.

Nearly nine years later, Packer was arrested near Fort Fetterman, Wyoming, and taken to Lake City, Colorado, for trial. In April 1883, he was found guilty of cannibalizing his companions and sentenced to hang the following month. An angry mob was ready to lynch Packer, so he was moved to the Gunnison jail for safekeeping. Legal technicalities kept him from the hangman's noose for more than three years, after which he was again tried, this time in Gunnison. The second jury found him guilty of five counts of manslaughter and sentenced him to forty years in the Colorado State Prison at Canon City.

Packer had served almost fifteen years when Governor Charles S. Thomas pardoned him in January 1901. As part of the parole agreement, Packer was to move to Denver and live there for at least six years and nine months. Just before the deadline was up, in April 1907, Parker died and was buried in the nearby Littleton Cemetery.

CHAPTER TWENTY

CLAY ALLISON'S TROUBLE AT LAS ANIMAS
·1876·

Clay Allison and his brother, John, were pretty well-known around the small town of Las Animas, Colorado. Clay owned a ranch just a few miles south, in New Mexico Territory, and in those days before fences determined where a man's spread ended, he often allowed his cattle to wander across the border and graze on the high plains of southeastern Colorado. So the folks of Las Animas paid little attention when the Allisons walked into the Olympic Dance Hall on the village's main street on a cold December day in 1876.

The Allison boys were born troublemakers. Even though they had frequented the Olympic on numerous occasions and knew that the management required patrons to check their weapons, Clay and John just strolled up to the bar fully armed. They drank a few, then drank a few more, and before long the brothers were pretty tipsy, not to mention rowdy and boisterous. Other customers complained that the boys were stomping the toes of some of the dancers and generally making a nuisance of themselves. Someone sent for the law.

The sheriff at Las Animas, John Spear, was busy with other matters, so he sent a deputy, Charles Faber, to disarm the Allison boys. Sure, they were drunk, the sheriff acknowledged, but they never had caused trouble before. Just tell them to surrender their guns while they are in the bar, he told Faber, and pick them up on their way out of town.

Faber may or may not have known of the Allison boys' reputations. If he had, he probably would have been a little more careful about how he handled the situation that day at the Olympic. After all, Clay Allison in particular was known as quite a rounder. If the deputy didn't realize Clay had already killed several men, it wasn't Allison's fault, because he liked to brag to anyone who would listen.

The Allisons were from Tennessee. Born around 1841, Clay was just old enough to join the Confederate Army when the Civil War broke out. Serving under cavalry commander General Nathan Bedford Forrest, Allison was captured at Shiloh but soon escaped. After the war, he migrated to Texas, trailed cattle for a while with Charles Goodnight, and settled in New Mexico.

Clay reportedly killed his first man back in Tennessee, while he was on medical leave from the Confederate Army. Clay spied a Union officer snooping around his mother's farm and promptly shot him. After Clay arrived in New Mexico, he spearheaded an effort to hang an incarcerated murderer named Kennedy. Allison demonstrated his maniacal temperament when he cut off Kennedy's head and sported it in a local saloon. In 1874, he shot and killed a man at Clifton House, New Mexico, over a horse race. And in 1875, he was involved in a second lynching after which he gleefully dragged the body of the victim about the countryside.

Deputy Sheriff Faber entered the Olympic Dance Hall, walked over to the Allison brothers—who by now were extremely unruly—and asked them to surrender their pistols. Both men refused. Faber left the bar, and the Allisons probably enjoyed a good laugh at his expense.

But Faber was not through. He walked across the street to the Americana Hotel and grabbed a ten-gauge shotgun from behind the desk clerk's counter. Seeing two locals sitting in the hotel lobby, he approached them, explained the situation, and deputized them. The three men marched back across the street and entered the Olympic, where the Allisons were still drinking and terrifying the rest of the customers.

Faber walked in first. This time he did not ask Clay and John to surrender their arms. He simply pointed the shotgun at John, who was on the dance floor. Clay, at the bar with his back to the door, whirled around and drew his pistol at the same time. As Faber's first round splattered John's chest with buckshot, Clay fired at the lawman four times, hitting him once in the chest. Faber fired the second barrel at John, hitting him this time in the leg, and then sank to the floor, dead. Clay ran to the door and fired at the two rapidly disappearing special deputies, but missed.

John was carried to a doctor's office, where he miraculously recovered from his wounds. Clay was arrested by Sheriff Spear but later released on a ten-thousand-dollar bond. The smooth-talking Clay convinced a grand jury that he had killed Faber in self-defense, and the charges against him were dropped.

After the Las Animas affair, Clay Allison left his New Mexico ranch and wandered throughout the West. He visited Dodge City, lived at Hays City, Kansas, for a while, went to St. Louis, and finally ended up in Texas. There, in July 1887, while driving a freight wagon from Pecos, where he had gone to purchase supplies, he fell from the wagon and fractured his skull on the front wheel. He died shortly thereafter.

Colorado was often visited by outlaws of varying reputations, but Clay Allison, no doubt, was one of the most notorious.

CHAPTER TWENTY-ONE

THE BIRTH
OF LEADVILLE,
SILVER CAPITAL
· 1877 ·

W illiam H. Stevens, a well-known miner, thought he would look one last time at the diggings around California Gulch, in the Rockies west of Denver. Stevens knew gold had been discovered there back in 1860, when Abe Lee had set off a rush to the region after finding the precious metal in the creek bed at the bottom of the gulch. But the gold had petered out after only two years, and the small settlement of miners' shacks that had grown up around the diggings had been practically deserted now for nearly thirteen years.

Stevens failed to locate any new outcrops of gold, nor could he find any gold dust mixed with the sand of the creek. As he carefully scoured the stream bottom, he became curious about the dark sands and bedrock that underlay the stream and the gulch. Picking up a few pieces of the ore, he took it to the local assayer's office and found that the matrix was carbonate of lead, the parent rock of silver. Stevens's small sample was assayed to yield two and a half pounds of silver to the ton of ore, a fairly rich mixture.

Stevens's find set off a new rush to the region, only this time the thousands of prospectors who poured into the nearby mountains were looking for silver instead of gold. The surrounding countryside was loaded with silver. One new mine yielded more than $100,000 worth of the metal within a twenty-four hour period! In 1877, Leadville was established at an elevation of about ten thousand feet to accommodate the endless stream of miners who combed every square foot of the mountainous terrain in search of their fortunes. By the 1880s, the town had a population of 25,000 and was one of the richest communities in the United States.

Leadville grew rapidly, not only in its population and wealth, but in its cultural and religious institutions as well. In its prime, the town boasted seven churches representing all the major denominations of the times. A three-story theater that hosted operas as well as Shakespearian plays was the pride of the community. A photographic studio in the town was compared to those of New York. Two hotels, complete with wonderful dining rooms—one of them supervised by a former chef at New York's Delmonico's—kept busy with the tourist and business trade of the day.

Many famous people visited Leadville, among them the British savant, Oscar Wilde. Arriving in the West in 1882, Wilde visited several towns on his lecture tour. The subject of Wilde's lecture was aestheticism, defined by the dictionary as "the pursuit of the sensuously beautiful,"—a topic of no interest to many residents of Leadville. Nevertheless, the effeminate Wilde was well-received, and his performances were well-attended. Despite a warning from acquaintances in Denver that Leadville was "the toughest as well as the richest city in the world and that every man carried a revolver," the playwright managed not only to survive the visit, but to impress a few of the townspeople along the way.

To show their appreciation for Wilde's cultural enlightenments, several miners carried the Englishman deep into the Matchless Mine on the outskirts of town to feed him supper. Despite the fact that it was after two o'clock in the morning, and that before the feast was over several bottles of liquor had been consumed, Wilde reappeared at the surface in much better shape than most of the miners. When asked about his subterranean activities, Wilde responded, "Having got into the heart of the mountain, I had supper, the first course being whiskey, the second whiskey, and the third whiskey."

After just a few years of outstanding silver production, the mines around Leadville began to peter out, just as the gold fields had a few years earlier. For a while, it appeared that Leadville would become a ghost town, like scores of other Rocky Mountain villages. But then, just when all hope was thought to be gone, the value of copper and zinc became known. Since both metals were common in the complex matrix that made up the rocky terrain around Leadville, a new era of progress and wealth opened for the tenacious little town and its people.

By 1895, Leadville was still boasting of its economic and scenic attributes to all who would listen. In an effort to draw attention to the region, the town fathers decided to build a gigantic "ice palace" to serve as the main attraction of a well-publicized winter carnival.

For two months, more than 250 craftsmen worked furiously to build the castle. Ice blocks that measured twenty by thirty inches were cut from nearby lakes and hauled overland to the construction site. After the blocks were placed side by side, they were sprinkled with water, which froze and converted the individual blocks into solid walls of ice. The buttressed walls measured 325 feet long, and the corners of the palace were dominated by solid ice towers complete with turrets. Inside was a skating rink that measured 190 by 80 feet. But all good things must come to an end, and by mid-June 1896, the ice palace had melted away, just like the good old days of Leadville.

CHAPTER TWENTY-TWO

UNCLE DICK WOOTTON'S TOLL ROAD
· 1878 ·

After spending more than four decades in the Wild West, Richens Lacy Wootton—mountain man, trader, rancher, and Indian fighter—was about to embark on a new career. The six-foot, 220-pound former Virginian was now sixty-two years old, and as his last contribution to the opening of the West, he decided to build a road across Raton Pass, connecting Colorado and New Mexico.

The path across the pass that Wootton intended to improve was part of the mountain branch of the Santa Fe Trail. This particular section of the trail, used by Missouri and New Mexican traders since 1821, had always proved difficult for travelers—particularly those with wagons—because of its steep grades, high precipices, and almost impassable, rock-strewn approaches. In fact, the difficulty of getting through Raton Pass with wagons was the primary reason the alternative Cimarron Cutoff section of the Santa Fe Trail had been opened.

Wootton, affectionately called "Uncle Dick" by his friends and acquaintances, moved to the base of the Colorado side of Raton Pass, near Trinidad, in 1866. In his biography, *"Uncle Dick" Wootton*, by Howard Louis Conard, Wootton gave his reasons for wanting to build the road across the Raton:

I had been over the mountains so often, had in fact lived in them so many years, that I knew almost every available pass in Colorado and New Mexico, and understood just about how the travel ran, in various directions. I knew that the Raton Pass was a natural highway, connecting settlements already in existence, and destined to be a thoroughfare for other settlements, which would spring up in southeastern Colorado and northeastern New Mexico. Barlow and Sanderson, the proprietors of the Santa Fe stage line, were anxious to change their route, so as to pass through Trinidad, which had by this time become a point of some importance, and the freighters generally wanted to come through that way. How to get through the pass, was the problem, however, with all of them.

In his initial exploration of the surrounding mountains, Wootton found the situation exactly as he remembered it from years earlier, when he had frequented the area on numerous trading and trapping excursions. "A trail led through the canon, it is true," he told Conard, "but that was almost impassable for anything but saddle horses and pack animals at any time, and entirely impassable for wagon trains or stages in the winter time."

Wootton applied to both the Colorado and New Mexican governments for charters to build his road. When all was approved, he began his gigantic effort.

I had undertaken no light task, I can assure you. There were hillsides to cut down, rocks to blast and remove and bridges to build by the score. I built the road, however, and made it a good one too.... [M]y twenty-seven miles of turnpike, constituted a portion of an international thoroughfare.

To pay for the design and construction of his road, Uncle Dick charged travelers a toll to use it. The concept immediately ran into trouble as Wootton quickly discovered that he "had to deal with a great many people who seemed to think that they should be as free to travel over my well graded and bridged roadway, as they were to follow an ordinary cow path."

Wootton divided his potential customers into five categories: the stage company and its employees, the freighters, the military, the Mexicans, and the Indians. He wisely decided not to charge the Indians, and he got along well with the stage people, the soldiers, and the freighters. However, he lamented:

> My Mexican patrons were the hardest to get along with. Paying for the privilege of traveling over any road was something they were totally unused to, and they did not take to it kindly. They were pleased with my road and liked to travel over it until they reached the toll gate.

But Wootton persisted, sometimes resolving problems "through diplomacy, and sometimes... with a club." And business was good; Wootton reaped several thousands of dollars in revenue in the twelve-year period, 1866 to 1878, that he operated the toll road.

By 1878, the railroad had reached central Colorado. Two fierce competitors—the Atchinson, Topeka, and Santa Fe line and the Denver and Rio Grande—considered Uncle Dick's toll road over Raton Pass an excellent route for their own roads. Wootton was partial to the AT&SF because it planned to route its railroad through Trinidad. The D&RG intended to bypass the town. With Wootton's assistance, AT&SF engineers located their route first, and their company won the contest to put a railroad over Raton Pass linking Colorado and New Mexico.

Wootton retired from his toll-road activities after the railroad came through. In exchange for his assistance, the AT&SF gave

Uncle Dick and his family lifetime passes on the train. It also gave Wootton, his wife, and his invalid daughter lifetime pensions. Wootton's house at the old toll gate burned in 1888, but he and his family lived in a cabin on the property until 1891, when they moved to Trinidad.

Wootton died on August 21, 1893, and was buried in the Trinidad Catholic Cemetery. Since his arrival at Bent's Fort fifty-seven years earlier, Wootton had seen Colorado transformed from a vast wilderness frequented only by mountain men, Indians, and Santa Fe traders to a modern state of the Union, serviced by the railroad, electricity, and the telephone.

CHAPTER TWENTY-THREE

THE UTE AFFAIR
· 1879 ·

As the autumn of 1879 approached, Arvilla Meeker, wife of the government agent at the White River Agency in northwestern Colorado, was growing apprehensive. She couldn't quite put her finger on the problem, but the way the Indians had been acting toward her husband lately sent chills through her.

Nathan C. Meeker, the man in charge of the Ute Indian reservation at White River, was a poor choice for the job, to say the least. Advanced in age, extremely idealistic, and a utopian at heart, Meeker had only a few years earlier led a brigade of bright-eyed visionaries in settling the town of Greeley, Colorado. The former agricultural editor of Horace Greeley's *New York Tribune*, Meeker intended to convert the harsh, dry prairie around Greeley into a farmer's paradise by introducing the concept of irrigation to the mixed bag of farmers he brought with him.

Although his project fared well after years of perseverance, Meeker's disciples had their doubts at times. "Who are all these people?" asked one of his associates not long after they had begun their long journey across the Great Plains. And why had they "gathered together under the leadership of one visionary old man, in the vain-hope of building up a paradise in the sands of the desert?"

While Meeker was busy with his Greeley project, silver was discovered along the Colorado River on the new Ute reservation in the western part of the state. Immediately, prospectors and miners pushed the Indians to give up their land and move yet again, this time to Indian Territory in what is now Oklahoma. It was at this point that Meeker got involved in the dispute.

Meeker, coming from a strong agricultural background, believed that the acceptance of farming by the Indians was the answer to the problem. With absolutely no empathy for the Utes' hunting traditions, the newly appointed agent initiated a campaign to convert these proud and abused people to an agricultural economy.

Only one problem marred this idealistic scenario. The Utes simply were not interested in farming. In September 1879, when Meeker demanded that the local Utes plow up a sizable meadow in which many of the Indians' horses grazed, the die was cast for the Utes. An embittered Meeker told one brave, an important medicine man, that he had too many horses anyway and that he "had better kill some of them." The Indian threw Meeker out the front door of the agency building and angrily left.

Meeker sent news of the affair to the authorities, and the incident provided Army officials with an excuse to send troops to the "relief" of the White River Agency. Major Thomas T. Thornburgh and a combined force of 175 infantrymen and cavalrymen left Fort Fred Steele, in nearby Wyoming, in mid-September.

The swift reaction and the imminent approach of Major Thornburgh's troopers caused consternation among the Utes. They were going to be forcibly removed from their reservation and sent packing to Indian Territory, they thought. But not without a fight!

Fearing more trouble than he could handle, Agent Meeker rode out to intercept the soldiers and asked Thornburgh to come to the agency for a council. When Thornburgh crossed onto the reservation with about 120 of his men, he found that his way was blocked by angry Utes, led by Chief Jack. A shot was fired, and the Battle of Milk Creek began. Thornburgh was killed immediately, but his second in command, Captain J. Scott Payne, reassembled the confused soldiers on the far side of the creek.

Over time, the Utes shot and killed all the soldiers' horses. They laid siege to the small contingent and waited while starvation slowly wore down the soldiers' resolve. The siege lasted nearly a week, but the captain had managed to send two messengers through the lines to gather help. A troop of the Ninth Cavalry came to the rescue, followed shortly by a larger force. When casualties were counted, sixty-one soldiers had been killed or wounded.

When the soldiers arrived at the agency some days later, they discovered that the Utes had beat them there. Nathan Meeker and nine other employees were dead. Mrs. Meeker, the couple's daughter, Josephine, and a Mrs. Price and her two children had been taken captive. Twenty-three days later, the women and children were released. Josephine Meeker lost no time in publicizing the event; a Philadelphia publisher released her account of the ordeal in late 1879.

The Ute Affair, or as it was sometimes called, the Meeker Massacre, was one more nail in the coffin for the Utes of northwestern Colorado. Efforts intensified to have the Indians thrown off their reservation, efforts which eventually succeeded. The various Ute bands were resettled in the extreme southwestern section of Colorado and in Utah.

Nathan Meeker was not totally responsible for the raw deal given the Utes. But his ignorance of the lifestyle and traditions of the Indians went a long way toward precipitating the gross misunderstanding between the two peoples. As one of the former Ute agents, Charles Adams, reported:

> I don't think that Mr. Meeker understood those Indians. He was a great agriculturalist, and he thought he could succeed in forcing the Indians to work and to accept the situation as farmers, but he did not take into consideration that it is almost impossible to force Indians into that sort of labor all at once.

Nathan Meeker paid dearly for his mistakes. He lost his life, his wife and daughter were taken into captivity, and many U.S. soldiers were killed. The Utes suffered, too. They not only lost a number of warriors in battle, but they were forced to pay outrageous annuities to the families of those killed in the massacre. And they lost the last of their original homeland forever.

CHAPTER TWENTY-FOUR

THE INHERITANCE OF OURAY
· 1880 ·

Ouray, the celebrated chief of the Utes, was around sixty years old in 1880, when the chronic kidney problems from which he had been suffering for some time caught up with him. With his wife, Chipeta, by his side, the mild-mannered warrior said his farewells, and in a brief time he was gone. As a last request, he asked his wife to keep the place of his burial a secret.

Some authorities believe Ouray was born in Colorado around 1820; others write that his birthplace was near Taos, New Mexico, and that his father was Ute but his mother was a Jacarilla Apache. In any event, he was raised in Colorado as a Ute, and when his father, who was chief of the tribe, died around 1860, Ouray inherited the job.

Ouray was a good choice for the number one spot in his tribe. He spoke fluent English, Spanish, and of course Ute. He chose to live much like a white man, and he and his wife maintained a sizable ranch complete with horses, livestock, and farm hands. Although Ouray had once been at odds with the white newcomers to his land, he had come to reconcile himself to the fact that the whites were here to stay. To survive, the chief simply threw in his lot with the invaders and tried to convert his people to the white man's lifestyle.

When Ouray assumed the role of chief, his people were spread over a great portion of western Colorado and eastern Utah. The Utes were a division of the Shoshonean group and were kin to the Paiute, Bannock, and Shoshone tribes. Although the Utes were usually at peace with the whites during Ouray's tenure as chief, this was not always the case.

On Christmas Day, 1854, a band of Utes mixed with a few Apaches attacked the Colorado settlement that one day would become Pueblo. Killing several whites, the Indians stole all the livestock and captured two women before raiding a settlement near today's Alamosa. Troops from Fort Union, New Mexico, strengthened by New Mexican volunteers, chased the renegade Indians across southern Colorado during the spring of 1855. In late April, the soldiers attacked two separate groups of Ute warriors and soundly defeated them. Devastated, the Indians sued for peace.

Over the years, a series of confusing and conflicting treaties had preserved for the Utes a fairly large reservation in Colorado and Utah. But many of the tribe's traditions stemmed from the buffalo-hunting culture of the Great Plains. Although Ouray was quick to adopt many of the white man's ways, large numbers of his kinsmen steadfastly refused to become farmers just to satisfy the government agents.

The sad events described in the previous chapter might have been avoided had Ouray been present. After all, as one historian wrote, Ouray was "noted chiefly for his unwavering friendship for the whites, with whom he always kept faith and whose interests he protected as far as possible, even on trying occasions."

But at the time of the Meeker Massacre, Ouray was away from the agency, and during his absence the strong influence that he normally had over other members of his tribe was not enough to prevent the tragedy. Still, when he returned, he moved quickly to quell the troubles. The historian continued:

> It was in all probability his firm stand and the restraint he imposed upon his people that prevented the spread of the outbreak of the Ute in Sept. 1879, when agent N. C. Meeker and others were killed and the women of the agency made captives. As soon as Ouray heard of this outbreak he commanded the cessation of hostilities, which the agent claimed would have stopped further outrage had the soldiers been withheld.

For his efforts at stopping the rebellion that occurred at White River, Chief Ouray was awarded an annuity of one thousand dollars a year by a grateful U.S. government. Unfortunately, the peacemaking chief lived less than a year after the event.

Ouray's faithful wife kept her promise and buried her husband in a secret place that was not revealed until 1924, some forty-four years after his death. The original burial site is now known to have been south of Ignacio, on the Ute Reservation. In 1925, the chief's body was moved to Montrose.

Ouray was a man for all seasons. At a time when white men looked possessively at the vast tribal lands held by the Utes, and the Utes were quick to retaliate for real and imagined wrongs, Ouray was a steadying voice in a world of chaos. His level-headed leadership no doubt saved countless lives, both Indian and white.

Ouray is remembered today with a stained-glass portrait in the dome of the State Capitol in Denver.

CHAPTER TWENTY-FIVE

THE WETHERILL BROTHERS AND MESA VERDE
· 1887 ·

In his autobiography, published posthumously in 1977, Benjamin Alfred (Al) Wetherill admitted he was not sure when he graduated from cowboy to archaeologist. He had always been interested in Indian lore and the many artifacts he found as he herded his family's cattle through the complex canyons of what is now Mesa Verde National Park. And he and his brothers had often listened to tales told by local Indians of the numerous "lost"

cities that still existed high in the cliffs of those same canyons. But though such things interested him immensely, he and the other boys had work to do and could spare little time to explore for ancient Indian villages.

Still, from time to time, Al and his brothers quizzed their Indian neighbors about the towns. The Wetherills always received the same tersely worded reply—actually a warning—that they would die if they ever found any of the ruins. What is more, the Indians themselves would be visited by death if they ever revealed the locations of any of the towns to white men. So, for years, the Wetherills drove their cattle through the deep canyons of Mesa Verde, never catching a glimpse of the legendary cliff dwellings.

One day in 1885, according to Al's autobiography, *The Wetherills of Mesa Verde,* the Wetherills were scouting among the canyons:

> Half-a-mile or so from where I came into the canon, I looked up and saw, under an overhanging cliff, a great cavernlike place in which was situated what seemed like a small ruined city. In the dusk and the silence, the great blue vault hung above me like a mirage. The solemn grandeur of the outlines was breathtaking. My mind wanted to go up to it, but my legs refused to cooperate. At the time I was so tired that I thought later would be the time for closer investigation. Keeping on down the canon was easy, but if I could have realized the extent of the find I had nearly made, I would not have been the least bit tired any more. My strength had waned to such an extent that I passed it by, not knowing what a great thing of archaelogical value I was overlooking.

When Al rejoined his companions, he told them about the vast ruin he had spotted from the canyon floor. But it was late and everyone was tired, and the group went back to the ranch house for the night. In time, Al forgot what he had seen.

Al did not realize at the time that he had viewed—supposedly for the first time ever by a white man—the famous Anasazi dwellings that would later become known as the Cliff Palace. Although the Dominguez-Escalante Expedition had passed within a stone's throw of the extensive ruins in 1776, the two churchmen had made no mention in their journals of exploring, or even seeing, such a place. And the eminent photographer William Henry Jackson had barely bypassed the ruins in 1874, when he was in the area with the Hayden Expedition.

It was not until 1888, when Al's brother Richard and their brother-in-law, Charles Mason, were riding through the canyons of Mesa Verde looking for cattle, that the Cliff Palace was again "discovered." Al wrote:

> Remembering what I had told them, they were half-prepared for the immensity of the vision but then, as later, the feeling struck them that the eerie sight could not be a reality. The cattle got away, but the amazement at seeing a miniature city spread out before them never did.

Soon, the two Wetherills and Mason returned to the Cliff Palace to further investigate their wonderful find. After exploring its vast ruins, Al declared that it was indeed the most spectacular of all the cliff dwellings in Mesa Verde. It was

> built under an arched roof ninety feet high, ninety feet deep, and perhaps four hundred feet of front originally. In back of the series of rooms was an open space the entire length of the cavern that was filled with all sorts of trash, as well as burials and hidden pottery.... The unusually good work in the dressing of the building stones and the construction of the walls are the most distinguishing characteristics of Cliff Palace. The rooms

go up three to four stories tall and each room was an average of eight feet square.

Al and his family left Mesa Verde in 1902. The cattle business had turned sour, and he moved on to work in New Mexico. Later, in 1908, President Theodore Roosevelt appointed him postmaster of Gallup, New Mexico, and he stayed in that job for about eight years. Later, he moved to Arkansas and then to Oklahoma, where he died in 1950.

In June 1906, the U.S. Department of Interior made Mesa Verde a national park. Today, thousands of tourists visit the park annually and stand in awe before the Cliff Palace and the other ruins, staring breathlessly, just as the Wetherill brothers did so many years ago.

CHAPTER TWENTY-SIX

THE LEGACY OF JESSE JAMES
· 1892 ·

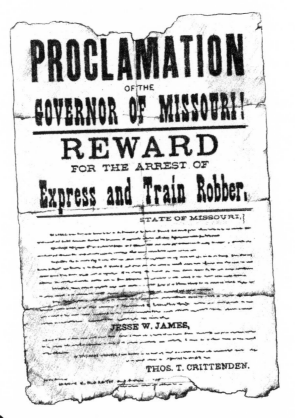

PROCLAMATION
OF THE
GOVERNOR OF MISSOURI!

REWARD
FOR THE ARREST OF
Express and Train Robber.

STATE OF MISSOURI,

JESSE W. JAMES,

THOS. T. CRITTENDEN.

Bob Ford was a tired man. Although he had only recently marked his thirtieth birthday, he felt much older. In the ten years since he had shot Jesse James, he had constantly been on the move. Everywhere he went, people jeered at him and called him names.

He did not understand it. He thought he had done the country a favor by killing its most infamous outlaw, and yet he was badgered constantly by an angry citizenry. They had loved the legends and mystery surrounding Jesse James. Now, with their hero gone, they made life miserable for Ford. Maybe here, in the wild mining town of Creede, Colorado, he could find some peace and quiet.

Ford opened a saloon in Creede, and for a while, it looked like he might at last find success. He and his wife, Dol, a former chorus girl, had moved to the wide-open town after the handsome Ford had failed in several other ventures, including the operation of a saloon in Las Vegas, New Mexico, and a stint in P.T. Barnum's freak show, where he had proudly told his story about the killing of Jesse James.

Ford often reflected on the day a decade ago when he had made his decision to murder James. Ford had made a deal with Thomas T. Crittenden, the governor of Missouri, to do James in for the ten-thousand-dollar reward the railroad companies had put up for the outlaw's capture or death. James was living in a house in St. Joseph at the time, and Ford, a minor member of the James gang, had no difficulty visiting him, since plans were being made for another robbery.

At about eight o'clock on the morning of April 3, 1882, James stood on a chair in his living room to straighten—or dust, depending upon which account is believed—a picture of the Confederate hero "Stonewall" Jackson. From about four feet away, Ford shot the outlaw multiple times in the back. Later, he claimed that the pistol "went off accidentally," but nevertheless he telegraphed Governor Crittenden that, "I have killed Jesse James."

The people of St. Joseph believed no man had the right to walk up behind another, outlaw or not, and shoot him pointblank in the back. The sheriff arrested Ford for murder. A jury quickly convicted him, but the governor pardoned him immediately. A public pariah, Ford soon left Missouri.

The shooting made front-page news in papers across the United States. The *Kansas City Daily Journal* headed its page-one article about the event with "Good Bye, Jesse!" Its series of subtitles continued:

> The Notorious Outlaw and Bandit, Jesse James, Killed at St. Joseph BY R. FORD, OF RAY COUNTY, A Young Man but Twenty-one Years of Age. THE DEADLY WEAPON USED Presented to His Slayer by His Victim but a Short Time Since. A ROBBERY CONTEMPLATED of a Bank at Platte City—To Have Taken Place Last Night. JESSE IN KANSAS CITY During the Past Year and Residing on One of the Principal Streets. KANSAS CITY EXCITED Over the Receipt of the News—Talks with People—Life of the Dead Man.

The competition, the *Kansas City Daily Times*, printed an extensive article that read in part:

> At a very early hour this morning, hundreds of people, men, women, and children began to wend their way toward the undertaker's establishment, where the dead body of the outlaw had been placed in a cooler, eager for a look at the noted train robber, and so dense was the throng at 9 o'clock that the doors had to be closed and a special detail of police called in to keep the tide of humanity back. The morbid curiosity of all classes was never more plainly shown than on this occasion, and as one man said, "I believe they would all come in the same way to see the devil."

Yes, Ford thought often of those long-ago days, and he never forgot that people still held him in contempt for what he had done.

One day in early June 1892, a former lawman named Edward ("Red") Kelly strolled into Ford's saloon in Creede and accused him of telling lies. Specifically, Kelly said, he had heard that Ford was spreading rumors around town that he, Kelly, had stolen Ford's diamond ring a few weeks earlier when the two had shared a hotel room in Pueblo. The two men scuffled, and Ford had Kelly thrown out of the saloon.

Kelly was a man known for his violent temper. Only a year earlier, he had killed a black man named Riley in Pueblo because the poor man had inadvertently stepped on his feet. Kelly was also believed to be a friend of the James family back in Missouri. Whatever his motivation, Kelly quickly acquired a shotgun, went back to Ford's saloon, and shot the owner dead.

Kelly was arrested for murder, convicted, and sentenced to the Colorado Prison at Canon City. Through the influence of friends in high places, he was paroled in 1902. Two years later, Kelly's temper got the best of him, and he was killed during a fight with an Oklahoma City policeman.

CHAPTER TWENTY-SEVEN

BARNEY FORD'S BLACK ACTIVISM
• 1902 •

Barney Ford did not know exactly what to expect when he arrived in Denver City on May 18, 1860. After all, the town was brand new. It had sprung up almost overnight when gold was discovered nearby. However, it did not take Ford long to realize that the one thing Denver did not have was very many blacks. Even here on the wild frontier, hundreds of miles from a nation headed for Civil War, feelings ran high over race, and Ford knew that the odds were stacked against him before he even reached the gold fields.

Ford had come to Denver from Chicago via Leavenworth, Kansas, where he was refused a stagecoach ticket. Undaunted, he took a job as a cook on a wagon train and reached Denver a little later than he had anticipated but still in high spirits. He never doubted that if thousands of other men could strike it rich prospecting and mining for gold, then he could, too. And that is exactly what Ford set out to do.

Ford filed two gold claims, but before he found out whether they would produce, he got kicked off his property because of a territorial law that prohibited blacks from filing land claims. A disastrous partnership with a white lawyer in a mine at Breckenridge, Colorado, sent the dejected Ford back to Denver, where he got a job as a bellboy at the Hemenway Hotel. When he had saved enough money, he sent to Chicago for his wife and son.

Ford soon opened a barbershop in the main section of rapidly growing Denver. His patrons were many of the town's leading citizens, and he became friends with most of the businessmen in the area. Soon after deciding not to join the Union Army because of family obligations, Ford lost his livelihood when his barbershop and home were accidentally destroyed by fire. Borrowing five thousand dollars from a German banker named Luther Kountze, Ford then opened the People's Restaurant. It was a fine establishment, and it drew its clientele from among the town's most respected citizens.

As the Civil War wound down in the East, Ford's thoughts turned more and more often to the plight of the black man in Colorado. Blacks in the United States still could not vote, and as increasing numbers of ex-slaves made their way westward, they were still treated like second-class citizens. Ford decided it was time to do something about the intolerable situation.

He went to Washington, D.C., at his own expense and lobbied Congress to defeat the 1864 statehood bill. The bill would have allowed Colorado to enter the Union as a free state, but it extended no rights to blacks. The bill was defeated, and Ford returned home to Denver to help establish adult-education classes for blacks and to organize the Colored Republican Club. Despite all his hard labor, no significant rights were given to Colorado's black population.

In 1867, Ford opened a second restaurant in Cheyenne. He managed both with a great deal of success. Fire eventually destroyed the Cheyenne business, but even with that financial setback, his personal worth was rumored to be more than $250,000. He was without doubt the wealthiest black man in Colorado.

Ford continued to be successful. He built the Ford House Hotel and People's Restaurant and the Inter-Ocean Hotel in Denver, as well as a mansion in the heart of the city.

In 1873, Ford became the first black man in Colorado history to run for public office. He was defeated in his bid for a seat in the Territorial Legislature.

By 1879, the fifty-seven-year-old Ford had just about lost his entire fortune. Another hotel in Cheyenne had failed, the cattle trade that supported his operations was drying up, and the economy was generally in a bad state of affairs. The following year, after unsuccessfully trying his luck in the California gold fields, Ford went to Breckenridge, penniless. There, he opened a restaurant for miners and slowly began to rebuild his fortune. He operated the Oyster Ocean Restaurant in Denver for a while and earned enough money to build a summer home in the nearby mountains.

In 1885, Ford was instrumental in getting a civil-rights law passed in Colorado that forbade the denial of equal rights to blacks in hotels, restaurants, and other public places. Two years later, he sold his share of a Breckenridge gold mine for a small fortune and found himself on top of the world again. Although financially secure, he opened another barbershop near the Brown Palace Hotel and continued to work.

From a slave's life in ante-bellum Georgia, Ford had come a long way. His entrepreneurial spirit provided budding Denver with badly needed businesses to supply the demands of its rapidly growing population. His drive to help his fellow blacks was directly responsible for much of the civil-rights legislation that eventually gave his brethren in the state equal opportunities. Ford died in 1902, no doubt with a sense of accomplishment.

CHAPTER TWENTY-EIGHT

MOTHER JONES'S UNION STAND
· 1913 ·

On a sunny day in September 1913, Mary Harris Jones, eighty-three years old and still feisty, stepped from the train at the station in Trinidad, Colorado. She was known affectionately throughout the labor world as "Mother Jones," but once she had been dubbed "the most dangerous woman in America" by a prosecutor in the West Virginia coal fields.

Mother Jones had come to Trinidad at the request of local coal miners who wanted her to assist them in organizing a strike against the Colorado Fuel and Iron Company, a large and powerful outfit controlled by John D. Rockefeller. Almost before her feet hit the station platform, Mother Jones began receiving warnings to leave town.

"They are sending me all sorts of threats here," she wrote to some friends in Washington, D.C. "They have my skull drawn and two cross sticks beneath my jaw to tell me that if I do not quit they are going to get me."

Jones found living and working conditions for the Colorado miners and their families to be primitive and unhealthy beyond belief. But this came as no surprise to her, since the majority of her life had been spent in helping labor movements, unions, and individuals fight large corporations for better working conditions, fair pay, and decent working hours. She had even been to Colorado several years earlier, when the president of the United Mine Workers asked her to check personally on labor conditions there.

On that earlier occasion, martial law had been declared, strikers had been arrested and thrown into open-air stockades, and free speech and assembly had been permitted only with the blessing of the state militia. One of the posters published by the mine workers' union read:

Martial Law declared in Colorado! Habeas Corpus suspended in Colorado! Free Press throttled in Colorado! Bull-Pens for Union Men in Colorado! Free Speech denied in Colorado! Soldiers defy the Courts in Colorado! Wholesale arrests without Warrant in Colorado! Union Men exiled from homes and families in Colorado! Constitutional right to bear arms questioned in Colorado.... IS COLORADO IN AMERICA?

Now here she was, a decade later, in Colorado again. And from all appearances, little had changed for the better since her earlier visit. She found the miners and their families living under the same squalid conditions, the company stores charging the same outrageous prices for food and other necessities. And she heard of frequent outbreaks of typhoid and other diseases caused by the filthy environment.

A few days after Mother Jones's arrival in Trinidad, a general strike was called among coal miners in southern Colorado. The Colorado Fuel and Iron Company called on a group of deputy sheriffs to protect its interests and to intimidate the strikers. During the strike's first week, Jones quickly found out what she and her cohorts were up against.

Rockefeller's company outfitted an armored car with a machine gun and proceeded to a miners' camp near the town of Forbes. *Harper's Weekly* told what happened next:

> [The car] stopped just a short distance from the Camp and one of the men took a white handkerchief, put it on the end of a stick and using it as a flag of truce approached the group of strikers. As he came up he asked if they were Union men, and receiving their reply in the affirmative, he threw down the flag, jumped to one side and said, "Look out for yourselves." At that the machine gun cut loose on the crowd. One hundred and forty-seven bullets were put through one tent; a boy 15 years old was shot 9 times in the legs; one miner was killed, shot through the forehead. This was but one of a series of incidents.

The national guard was finally brought in to control the violence, but it soon became evident that the militia had no intention of going head to head with the Colorado Fuel and Iron Company. Conditions were no better under martial law than they were before. Miners and their families were still abused, only now the abuse had official blessing.

Termed a "dangerous rabble-rouser" by the commander of the national guard, Jones was finally jailed without a hearing and with no charges filed against her. She smuggled a letter out of her prison cell, and newspapers all over the country printed it on page one. In part, the letter read:

> I am being held a prisoner incommunicado in a damp underground cell.... I want to say to the public that I am an American citizen... and I claim the right of an American citizen to go where I please so long as I do not violate the law.... [N]ot even my incarceration... will make me give up the fight in which I am engaged for liberty and for the rights of the working people. To be shut from the sunlight is not pleasant but... I shall stand firm. To be in prison is no disgrace.

Jones finally was pressured into leaving Colorado. She went directly to Washington, D.C., to testify before Congress about the inhumane treatment of the miners by the big companies. In the meantime, the killings and abuses in Colorado continued. When the federal government finally sent troops to quell the violence, Jones returned to Denver, declaring to a huge crowd that "Washington is aroused and there is help coming."

Jones died in 1930 at the age of 103, before the passage of a federal law allowing workers the right to form unions. The legislation was a belated tribute to a woman who, for sixty years, fought tooth and nail for the American worker. She was loved and revered by thousands of men and women of the laboring class. One of them, deeply touched by his mentor's death, wrote the following:

> The world today is mourning
> The death of Mother Jones
> Grief and sorrow hover
> Around the miners' homes.
> This grand old champion of labor
> Has gone to a better land,
> But the hard-working miners,
> They miss her guiding hand.

CHAPTER TWENTY-NINE

THE DEATH OF BUFFALO BILL
· 1917 ·

It was January 10, 1917. War was raging in Europe, and the United States was just weeks away from entering the conflict. Woodrow Wilson was about to embark on his second term as president after barely defeating his opponent, Charles Evans Hughes, in the November election. General John J. ("Black Jack") Pershing was off in the hinterlands of Mexico chasing the bandit, Pancho Villa. And in Denver, Colorado, one of the greatest showmen in the world, Colonel William F. ("Buffalo Bill") Cody, lay dying.

Cody had returned to the West after performing for the last time in his spectacular Wild West show at Portsmouth, Virginia, in November 1916. His doctor had hoped the mineral waters at a Colorado sanitarium would improve his health, but they did little good. So he moved to the home of his sister, Mrs. May Decker, in Denver.

When the doctor announced that Cody had no more than thirty-six hours to live, the old performer called his brother-in-law to his bedside to play cards. On January 10, 1917, Buffalo Bill died. In those last few hours, amid the pain of kidney, heart, and prostate failures, Cody must have reminisced about his fabulous career, a lifetime of adventure that started in 1846 as the United States went to war with Mexico.

As a youngster, Cody worked for a freighting company as an express messenger. A brief stint with the Pony Express provided the future showman with plenty of material for his Wild West shows. The Civil War found sixteen-year-old Cody riding as a scout with the Ninth Kansas Volunteers, and later the boy joined the Seventh Kansas Cavalry as a private.

After the war, Cody caught the eye of General Philip H. Sheridan, who hired him as chief of scouts for the Fifth U.S. Cavalry, a job he held from 1868 until 1872. Cody was present at the Army's defeat of the Cheyennes at Summit Springs, Colorado, in July 1869, and during his career he fought in numerous other Indian battles. During this period, one of his superiors remarked that Cody provided "extraordinarily good services as trailer and fighter" and added that "his marksmanship being very conspicuous... I hope to be able to retain him as long as I am engaged in this duty."

Around 1869, the dime novelist Ned Buntline (Edward C. Judson), published a small book in which Cody, who by then was already known as Buffalo Bill, was the main character. The book was successful and was eventually made into a play in which Cody himself appeared in Chicago. He added to his fame by guiding government-sponsored foreign dignitaries on hunting trips across the Great Plains and in the Rocky Mountains. For several years thereafter, he divided his time between scouting and acting.

Eventually sickening of the stage, Cody returned to the West. The Sioux and Cheyenne had just defeated Custer and his Seventh Cavalry at the Battle of the Little Bighorn. Several days later, Cody became involved in an incident that guaranteed his place in American legend. While Cody was riding with the Fifth Cavalry in Nebraska, a small group of Cheyenne warriors approached, and one of them, a chief named Yellow Hair, more or less challenged Cody to a fight. Buffalo Bill won, killed Yellow Hair, scalped him in front of his speechless companions, and held the scalp high above his head while screaming, "First scalp for Custer!"

But the show-business bug had bitten Cody, and in 1883 he organized his first Wild West tour. Cody was no businessman, however, and his lack of day-to-day managerial skills, added to his increasing reliance on alcohol, placed the show in jeopardy. An infusion of new cash revived the tour, and in 1885 Annie Oakley and Sitting Bull were added to the roster of performers. The public loved it.

Cody took his show all over the United States and Europe. He and his troupe performed before Queen Victoria and other foreign heads of state. In France, the crowds yelled "Vive Annee Oaklee!" as the rifle-toting woman amazed them with her marksmanship. Cody's extravaganza was just as well-received in Italy, Germany, and Spain. In fact, Europeans loved the lore of the West as much if not more than Americans, and they eagerly sought out Buffalo Bill's entourage wherever it went.

Back in the United States, Cody's show was seen by more than six million spectators at the Chicago World's Columbian Exposition in 1893. Cody and his business associates made hundreds of thousands of dollars, but in the end, Cody lost it all. When he established the town of Cody, Wyoming, the cost drained hlm financially. He went deeper into debt when some ill-planned mining investments failed.

Cody still had his show, however, and he plodded along with it for a few more years. A large debt to the co-owner of *The Denver Post*, Harry H. Tammen, eventually sealed Cody's fate, and his show slowly died, forcing him to become an employee of Tammen's own half-baked circus. Finally, after threatening to shoot Tammen, Cody "persuaded" his adversary to forgive the debt.

But it was too late for a comeback. Severely ill, Cody continued to make every performance until that last night in Portsmouth, after which he had to return West. From that point on, it was just a matter of time until his terminal maladies caught up with him.

Much of Denver turned out for Buffalo Bill's funeral. His body lay in state in the rotunda of the State Capitol building, and more than 25,000 people watched as his funeral procession wound through the city streets. His old pal Teddy Roosevelt, as well as President Woodrow Wilson, sent their condolences.

Even in death, however, Cody had his problems. He had left instructions to be buried in the town of his own creation, Cody, Wyoming. But there was not enough money to fulfill his wish. Cody's old enemy, Harry Tammen, stepped in and announced that Buffalo Bill should be buried atop Lookout Mountain, west of Denver.

Five months after his death, amid an almost carnival atmosphere, Cody was finally buried, not in the place he wished, but at least in the mountains he loved and among people who adored him. The man who made the Wild West come alive for so many people rests there today in a peace that eluded him in life.

CHAPTER THIRTY

THE LEGEND OF BABY DOE
· 1935 ·

In March 1935, her emaciated body was found frozen to the rough-planked floor of a tool shack at the Matchless Mine in Leadville, Colorado. The local doctor was called, and he declared that the woman had been dead for about two weeks. The winter's intense cold had preserved her body so that even her facial features could still be discerned.

As news of the gruesome discovery spread through Leadville, a crowd soon gathered outside the mining shack. Curious onlookers exchanged whispers as the body was transported through the deep snow to an awaiting hearse. For some of them, the woman's death brought to mind a poignant, yet ironic, tale.

The woman was Elizabeth McCourt Doe Tabor, and she was the widow of Horace Tabor, who during the early 1880s had been the wealthiest man in Colorado. Elizabeth, known in her heyday as "Baby Doe," was Tabor's second wife, and the story was that he had deserted his first spouse, Augusta, for this beautiful divorcee twenty-four years his junior.

Horace had been quite a fixture in both Leadville and Denver during the old days. A native of Vermont, he and Augusta had immigrated to Colorado in 1857. Like so many other easterners of the times, they had dreamed of striking it rich somewhere in the vast gold and silver fields of the American West.

Tabor's early success came not as a prospector but as a merchant, filling the equipment and supply needs for other miners. It was while he was in this business that a pair of worn-out prospectors begged him for seventeen dollars worth of supplies in exchange for a one-third share of their as yet unproductive silver mine. Reluctant but compassionate, Tabor gave in and furnished the men with the needed supplies. Shortly afterwards, the two struck a silver vein, and soon it was producing twenty thousand dollars worth of ore a week. A year later, Tabor made his first million when he sold his share in the mine.

From then on, the story of the Tabors was one of rags to riches. Everything Horace touched turned to money. He bought a mansion in Denver, hired servants for his disbelieving wife, and invested heavily in scores of schemes. By 1881, Tabor was worth an estimated nine million dollars, and his fortune was still growing. He built an opera house in Denver, as well as the five-storied Windsor Hotel, as fine as any hostelry in New York or San Francisco.

And he discovered Baby Doe.

Denver socialites were shocked when they learned that Horace Tabor had dumped his faithful wife of twenty-five years for the lovely Elizabeth. But Horace was not the only one smitten by the divorcee. A newspaper article of the day declared that she was

without doubt the handsomest woman in Colorado. She is young, tall, and well-proportioned, with a complexion so clear that it reminds one of the rose blush mingling with the pure white lily; a great wealth of light brown hair, large, dreamy blue eyes, and a shoulder and bust that no Colorado Venus can compare with.

By 1883, Horace had settled with Augusta for $300,000, and the pair parted ways. While the divorce was still in the Denver courts, Tabor was sent to Washington, D.C., by his Republican cronies to serve a thirty-day term in a U.S. Senate seat that had been recently vacated. Tabor took Baby Doe with him, and when the divorce became final, he married her at the Willard Hotel on Pennsylvania Avenue. Among the guests awed by Baby Doe's seven-thousand-dollar wedding dress and ninety-thousand-dollar diamond necklace was President Chester A. Arthur, who remarked, "I have never seen a more beautiful bride."

Tabor ran for a seat in the U.S. Senate in 1886 and tried for the Colorado governorship in 1888. Both positions eluded him, and some political critics said his extramarital escapade was the reason. Fortunately for Horace, his political failures were not matched by financial ones. He kept spending money, most of it on unwise investments. Change was in the air, however, and the financial Panic of 1893, coupled with the repeal of the Sherman Silver Purchase Act, gradually drove the Tabors out of business.

Horace Tabor lost it all. To make ends meet, he disposed of his houses, his mines, and his stables and horses. He even sold all Baby Doe's jewelry and furs. In 1898, sympathetic Republican friends got him the job of postmaster of Denver, but the following year the flamboyant "king of the silver mines" died penniless.

The only silver mine Tabor had retained during his lean years was the Matchless, just outside Leadville. Some say than on his deathbed, he told Baby Doe to keep the property as long as she could. After the funeral, the bereaved widow traveled to Leadville, moved into the vacant tool shed beside the opening to the main shaft, and lived out the rest of her days in poverty, dreaming of the time when the petered-out mine would once again make her the belle of Denver society.

CHAPTER THIRTY-ONE

W. H. JACKSON'S QUEST FOR THE CROSS

· 1942 ·

Although it was late August, the high Rocky Mountains through which photographer William Henry Jackson and his associates tramped that day in 1873 were shrouded in freezing mist and snow. The men's goal was to sight the famed "Mountain of the Holy Cross," an enigma that had eluded adventurers since the early days of exploration in the Colorado Rockies.

Prospectors and mountain men had talked about the mountain for years, but no one had ever been able to get close enough to unravel its mystery. From a distance, the most anyone had been able to see were two great arms of snow forming a huge cross on one side of the precipice.

At the time of his ascent, Jackson was a member of the Hayden Survey party, which was mapping and photographing the Colorado Rockies. Jackson had left his office in Washington, D.C., in the early spring and made his way cross-country to Denver, arriving there in mid-May. He became excited when his associate on the survey, chief topographer J.T. Gardner, asked him if he had ever heard of the Mountain of the Holy Cross. When Jackson acknowledged that he had, Gardner replied, "Everybody talks about it and nobody sees it. I'd like to fix that. Hayden [the survey leader] doesn't know it yet, but I think we'll pay it a visit."

And now, here was Jackson at last. The mist was thick, and the cold was intense. Before he could set up his heavy camera equipment, the entire region became so socked in that it was impossible to take photographs. He decided he had waited all this time to see the mountain first-hand, so he could wait one more day.

The next day, August 24, saw Jackson and his men up early, ascending a nearby mountain from their base camp. It was still freezing cold, but the sun had risen and the sky was cloudless. After a breath-taking climb of fifteen hundred feet, the party finally reached the crest and looked out over a broad valley. And there at last was the object of their search! The Mountain of the Holy Cross was fully visible and looked exactly as the old-timers seeing it from a distance had described it.

Jackson quickly set up his equipment and spent the next few hours taking photographs of the legendary mountain. He was the first man ever to do so, and the image he captured that day has not faded. Thomas Moran, the great landscape artist, used Jackson's photo as the basis for his renowned painting of the mountain, and reproductions of the photograph itself circulated throughout the United States for years.

Several years after Jackson captured the mountain's beauty and majesty, a guidebook described the peak as

> renowned to the ends of the earth, and is the only one with this name in the world. It is the principal mountain of the Sawatch Range, just west of the Middle Park of Colorado, and exceedingly difficult of access.... The characteristic features which give it its name is the vertical face, nearly 3,000 feet in depth, with a cross at the upper portion, the entire fissures being filled with snow. The cross is of such remarkable size and distinct contrast with the dark granite rock, that it can be seen nearly eighty miles away, and easily distinguished from all other mountain peaks. The snow seems to have been caught in the fissure, which is formed of a succession of steps, and here, becoming well lodged, it remains all the year. Late in the summer the cross is very much diminished in size by the melting of the snow.... The height of the mountain is 14,176 feet above tide-water. The perpendicular arm of the cross is 1,500 feet in length, and fully 50 feet in breadth, the snow lying in the crevice from 50 to 100 feet in depth. The horizontal arm varies in length with the seasons, but averages 700 feet.

In 1879, Jackson opened a photographic studio in Denver and made the town his base of operations for twenty years. He and his family resided in several homes in the city, eventually ending up on fashionable Capitol Hill at 1430 Clarkson.

The Jacksons moved to Detroit in 1898, then to Washington, D.C., where, at the age of ninety-three, Jackson decorated the walls of the U.S. Department of the Interior with his paintings.

On June 30, 1942, Jackson died of injuries caused by a fall down the steps of a New York City hotel. The patriarch was ninety-nine years old, and his obituaries hailed him as one of the greatest photographers the United States had ever produced. Ironically, only eight years later, the Mountain of the Holy Cross, which had earlier been designated a national monument, lost its status as such due to warming temperatures that continuously melted the snow from the mountain's "cross."

CHAPTER THIRTY-TWO

THE SEARCH FOR BRIDEY MURPHY
· 1952 ·

As evening approached on Saturday, November 29, 1952, Morey Bernstein, a Pueblo, Colorado, businessman, began to get nervous. For several weeks, Bernstein had been hypnotizing a young, female acquaintance in an attempt to take her back to her childhood. The experiment had been going extremely well, and Bernstein had regressed the woman all the way back through her grammar school days to the time she was one year old.

Bernstein was optimistic about his work with the woman, whom he later called Ruth Simmons, a fictitious name used to protect her real identity. As he continued his experiments with her, he began to wonder if she could be taken back via hypnosis to a time before birth. Do human beings have any recollection of times and events before they were born? he wondered. Was there really any such thing as "reincarnation" or the "transmigration of souls?"

Bernstein's questions were answered to his satisfaction that November evening, when Ruth and her husband came to the hypnotist's home. This was the night Bernstein had chosen to try to take Ruth beyond birth and ask her about previous lives. To preserve his evidence, he recorded this session and those that followed on tape.

As Bernstein's wife and Ruth's husband watched, Bernstein hypnotized his subject and progressively carried her back in time to age seven, then five, then three, and finally one. Ruth answered all Bernstein's questions knowledgeably and candidly at each

117

age. Bernstein then softly told Ruth that he wanted her to continue to regress to whatever place and time her mind settled on. He explained that when she arrived at that place, she must tell him what appeared to her.

After a few tense moments, Ruth began to describe in a soft voice a time when she had scraped all the fresh paint from her metal bed. She said she had done it because she had just received a spanking from her mother. At Bernstein's prompting, Ruth said that her name was Bridey Murphy, that she was eight years old, that the year was 1806, and that she lived in Cork, Ireland!

As the evening progressed, Bernstein regressed Ruth beyond 1806 to another life when she was a baby in New Amsterdam. When he could get her no farther back in time, he brought her back to Ireland and resumed his questioning of her as Bridey Murphy. Ruth revealed that after she was grown, she married a man named Brian McCarthy. The childless couple later lived in Belfast, and she died on a Sunday at the age of sixty-six from injuries sustained in a fall down some stairs.

Over the next year, Bernstein put Ruth under hypnosis several more times. During each session, he asked and re-asked the same questions: what was her name, where did she live, what was her husband's name, when did she die? Never once did Ruth falter in her responses, and never once did she contradict herself. What's more, in her answers she used certain colloquialisms and anachronisms that neither Bernstein nor any of the witnesses understood. When these words and phrases were checked later, they were invariably found to have been commonly used in Ireland in the early to mid-nineteenth century.

Ruth, as Bridey Murphy, actually named businesses with which she and her family traded. She identified churches and schools. All these places were confirmed by independent investigators as legitimate landmarks.

Bernstein became a believer in reincarnation as a result of the Bridey Murphy interviews. An eminent British psychiatrist, Sir

Alexander Cannon, had written years before in his book, *The Power Within*:

> For years the theory of reincarnation was a nightmare to me, and I did my best to disprove it and even argued with my trance subjects to the effect that they were talking nonsense, and yet as the years went by one subject after another told me the same story in spite of different and varied conscious beliefs, in effect until now, well over a thousand cases have been so investigated I have to admit that there is such a thing as reincarnation.

Bernstein could not have agreed more with Dr. Cannon.

In 1956, Bernstein published his findings in a book entitled *The Search for Bridey Murphy*. The bestseller took the nation by storm. Predictably, with a subject as controversial as this, the book received both good and bad reviews. The scientific community, which had been wrestling with the question of reincarnation for years, for the most part maintained its old dogmatic ways. But Bernstein's book opened up a whole new interest in matters of the mind, and today the concept of reincarnation is much more widely accepted than it was in the 1950s.

CHAPTER THIRTY-THREE

RED RYDER AND LITTLE BEAVER
· 1960 ·

Few American men under the age of sixty-five did not at one time own—or long to own—a Daisy Red Ryder BB rifle. The gun was every boy's dream, and to be able to crank that lever and let go a round was like nothing else in the world. Probably more outlaws and renegade Indians died of blasts from Red Ryders in young imaginations than from all the rifles and pistols used during the real "winning" of the West.

The creative force behind the Daisy rifle was a lanky Colorado cowboy named Fred Harman. He was born in 1902 and moved from Missouri to the area around Pagosa Springs, Colorado, while he was still young. There, among the forested slopes of the Rocky Mountains, Fred's father and uncle started separate ranches.

Young Fred adapted to ranch life quickly. As a boy, he rode herd, branded, and performed all the other thousand and one chores required of a cowboy worth his salt. When he returned with his family to Kansas City in 1916, he got homesick for the range, and soon he went back to the Pagosa Springs area and got a job on a local ranch. But while Harman trailed cattle, another interest completely unrelated to the ranch life he loved kept gnawing at him. He had discovered that he possessed artistic talent, and in his spare time he would sketch the cowboys on the trail, the cattle, the horses, and the beautiful landscapes that surrounded him.

After almost a decade in the saddle, Harman decided it was time to develop his artistic skills. He left the ranch at Pagosa Springs and went to Kansas City. There, he obtained a job at the Film Ad Company, an outfit that produced animated cartoons. One of Harman's friends and co-workers was another young fellow who had a penchant for drawing—Walt Disney.

When Harman had learned all he could about cartooning at Film Ad, he moved on, and by 1927 he was working in St. Joseph, Missouri, as a catalog illustrator. The work was good, but it was not what Harman wanted. He wanted to be a cartoonist, but when that did not happen, he decided to go back to Colorado and do what he did best—punch cows. In 1933, he built a small log cabin near Pagosa Springs and, in addition to his ranch work, continued to improve his drawing and cartooning skills.

The next year, Harman, now thirty-two years old, entered some of his artwork in an exhibition at Los Angeles. His material was ignored. Later the same year, he created a cowboy cartoon character named "Bronc Peeler." At first, he was unable to interest a syndicate in his feature, but after he added a little Indian boy named "Little Beaver" to the comic strip, it became a success. Harman changed Bronc's name to "Red Ryder," and the phenomenally popular "Red Ryder and Little Beaver" comic strip was born.

Harman's Red Ryder feature was picked up in 1938 by the Newspaper Enterprise Association and syndicated to 750 newspapers across the country. At the peak of its popularity, the strip was read by some forty million Americans. It soon inspired ancillary products, such as a national radio show, several "Big Little Books," thirty-eight movies, more than forty other miscellaneous items, and finally, in the late 1940s, comic books. Harman's prosperity was assured.

In the late 1930s, with Red Ryder, Little Beaver, and Fred Harman already household names across America, Harman traveled to Plymouth, Michigan, to meet with the Daisy Air Rifle people. Daisy had been making air rifles, or "BB guns," for years. Harman wanted to interest them in manufacturing a BB version of a Colt single-action pistol, the kind Red Ryder carried in the comic strip. The people at Daisy thought the time was not right for a BB pistol, but they *were* interested in working with Harman on the design of an air rifle modeled after Red's Winchester lever-action carbine.

And so the Daisy Red Ryder air rifle was born. Millions of them were sold across the country during the 1940s and 1950s. Recently, Daisy introduced a fiftieth-anniversary version of the original Red Ryder rifle to commemorate the successful partnership of Daisy, Red Ryder, and Little Beaver.

In 1960, Harman decided to call it quits. Kids were not interested in playing cowboys and Indians anymore, and besides, after all those years of producing Red Ryder comics, he wanted to devote some time to fine painting. He was an immediate success. In 1965, when the Cowboy Artists of America group was formed, Harman became one of the original members. He wrote and illustrated a book, *The Great West Remembered*, which sold extremely well. He painted with a passion. He once said, "With my hair showing many winters, each morning before sun-up finds me hurriedly returning to my easel."

The man three generations of American boys can thank for the wonderful Red Ryder BB rifle died in 1982 on his spread near Pagosa Springs. Today, nearby, the Fred Harman Art Museum beckons travelers to step back in time and travel with Harman through his years as cowboy, cartoonist, fine artist, and portrayer of the real American West.

CHAPTER THIRTY-FOUR

THE HISTORY OF TWO HISTORIANS
· 1984/1985 ·

In 1930, a stranger approached Dr. Nolie Mumey on a downtown Denver street and asked for directions to the post office. The thirty-nine-year-old physician blushed as he told the inquirer that, although Denver had been his home for six years, he did not know where the post office was. This glaring lack of familiarity with his Colorado surroundings prompted Dr. Mumey to spend more than fifty years doing historical research.

Mumey (pronounced "mummy") was born in Shreveport, Louisiana, on February 8, 1891, and he received his medical degree from the University of Arkansas. But medicine was not his only interest. His other passions included flying, books, and history. And he found imaginative ways to tie those interests together.

After graduating from medical school, Mumey attended the University of Denver, where he received both a bachelor's and master's degree. His master's thesis was entitled, *A Study of Rare Books*, and it inaugurated a lifetime of writing. In 1931, Mumey published *The Life of Jim Baker*, a biography of a Colorado mountain man that still is recognized as the most authoritative source on its subject. Today, the book commands prices as high as $350 on the rare-book market. Over the next few years, Mumey's prolific pen produced books on such varied subjects as the early settlement of Denver, Calamity Jane, the history of the town of Creede, Poker Alice, Bent's Fort, the Pony Express, Jim Beckwourth, the founding of the University of Arkansas Medical

School, the evolution of flight, and physical requirements for commercial fliers.

Although writing took a great deal of his time, Dr. Mumey continued to practice medicine. At a 1952 American Medical Association meeting, he performed a thyroidectomy on closed-circuit television before 2,500 amazed onlookers. He became a flight surgeon in the Colorado National Guard and was the only physician in the organization who also held a pilot's license. From 1937 to 1969, he served as the company physician for Continental Airlines.

As Mumey approached his nineties, he still saw patients on a daily basis, and he continued to do so until a few months before his death on January 22, 1984. He was buried in the gown of a Fellow of the American College of Surgeons, an organization that he had served for the past fifty years.

In addition to Mumey, another man comes to mind when the topic of discussion is Colorado history. LeRoy R. Hafen was born at Bunkerville, Nevada, on December 8, 1893, and he graduated from Brigham Young University in Utah in 1916. He received his doctorate in history from the University of California at Berkeley, where he studied under the great historian Herbert Eugene Bolton.

Hafen gravitated to Colorado in 1923, where he took a job as state historian, curator of history at the Colorado Historical Society, and editor of *Colorado Magazine.* He held the position for nearly thirty years. During that time, he also penned such outstanding works as *Broken Hand: The Life Story of Thomas Fitzpatrick, Chief of the Mountain Men,* co-authored with William J. Ghent; *Fort Laramie and the Pageant of the West,* co-authored with Francis M. Young; and *Colorado, A Story of the State and Its People.*

Hafen's collaborator on much of his historical research, as well as on many of his books and magazine articles, was his wife, Ann Woodbury Hafen (1893-1970). A historian in her own right, she co-authored *Colorado, A Story of the State and Its People,* as well as several other works, including *Old Spanish Trail: Santa Fe to Los Angeles* and the extremely popular and informative *Handcarts to Zion: The Story of a Unique Western Migration, 1856-1860.*

The Hafens left Colorado in 1954 to return to Brigham Young University, where the couple continued their research and writing in earnest. It was during these years of "retirement" that the Hafens edited two monumental works for the Arthur H. Clark Company: *The Far West and the Rockies Historical Series, 1820-1875*, a fifteen-volume set published between 1954 and 1961; and *The Mountain Men and the Fur Trade of the Far West*, a ten-volume collection of biographies of nearly three hundred fur-trade luminaries.

Active until the end, Hafen died at his winter home in Palm Desert, California, on March 8, 1985.

Mumey and Hafen knew and respected each other. In fact, Hafen chose Dr. Mumey to write the biography of Jim Baker in his collection of mountain men and fur traders. The two men were both scholars, and both were devoted to the production of carefully researched and accurate, yet readable, history. Between the two, they wrote, co-wrote, or edited literally hundreds of books and magazine articles, many of them dealing with some aspect of Colorado history.

A POTPOURRI OF COLORADO FACTS

• Colorado is the eighth largest state in the nation after Alaska, Texas, California, Montana, New Mexico, Arizona, and Nevada. It encompasses 104,091 square miles, or almost 67 million acres. It averages 387 miles from east to west and 276 from north to south.

• The mean elevation of Colorado is 6,800 feet, making it the highest state in the nation. The highest point in the state is Mount Elbert, in Lake County, with an altitude of 14,433 feet. Colorado contains fifty-six peaks with altitudes exceeding fourteen thousand feet above sea level. The lowest point in the state (3,350 feet) is where the Arkansas River crosses the Colorado-Kansas border in Prowers County.

- The geographical center of Colorado is thirty miles northwest of Pikes Peak in Park County.

- The latest agricultural statistics (1991) show that Colorado contains approximately 26,000 farms totaling about 33 million acres, an average of 1,269 acres per farm.

- The 1990 Census reveals that Colorado has a population of 3,294,394 people, or 31.8 people per square mile. The state ranks twenty-sixth in the nation for population.

- The coldest temperature ever recorded in Colorado was minus sixty-one degrees Fahrenheit on February 1, 1985, at Maybell. The average low temperature in January is twenty-six degrees.

- The hottest temperature was 118 degrees on July 11, 1888, at Bennett. The average high temperature in July is seventy-three degrees.

- Colorado became a U.S. Territory in 1861. It became the thirty-eighth state on August 1, 1876.

- Denver is both the capital of Colorado and its largest city, with a population in 1990 of 467,610.

- Colorado contains sixty-three counties.

- The word Colorado is Spanish for "red."

- The state motto is *Nil sine numine*, which is Latin for "Nothing without providence."

- Colorado's official state nickname is "The Centennial State," because the state entered the Union in 1876, one hundred years after the signing of the Declaration of Independence.

- The state bird is the lark bunting (*Calamospiza melanocorys*), and the state mammal is the Rocky Mountain bighorn sheep (*Ovis canadensis*).

- The state flower is the blue columbine (*Aquilegia coerulea*), and the state tree is the blue spruce (*Picea pungens*).

- The state song is "Where the Columbines Grow."

- The state flag consists of a large red "C" surrounding a golden sphere, against a background of three horizontal stripes— blue, white, blue.

- Colorado is home to the Royal Gorge Bridge, the highest such structure in the world. The bridge was built in a record six months in 1929. It spans the Arkansas River at a height of 1,053 feet above the water.

Bibliography

Atkinson, Linda. *Mother Jones: The Most Dangerous Woman in America*, Crown Publishers, Inc., New York, 1978.

Bernstein, Morey. *The Search for Bridey Murphy*, Doubleday & Company, Inc., Garden City, New York, 1956.

Bird, Isabella L. *A Lady's Life in the Rocky Mountains*, University of Oklahoma Press, Norman, 1960. Reprinted by Comstock Editions, Sausalito, California, 1971.

Bonner, T. D. *The Life and Adventures of James P. Beckwourth*, Harper & Brothers, Publishers, New York, 1856.

Brewerton, George Douglas. *Overland with Kit Carson*, A. L. Burt Company, New York, n.d.

Briggs, Walter. *Without Noise of Arms*, Northland Press, Flagstaff, Arizona, 1976.

Conard, Howard Louis. *"Uncle Dick" Wootton*, W. E. Dibble & Co., Chicago, 1890. Reprinted by Time-Life Books, Alexandria, Virginia, 1980.

Coues, Elliott, ed. *The Journal of Jacob Fowler*, Ross & Haines, Inc., Minneapolis, 1965.

Crutchfield, James A. *The Santa Fe Trail*, due to be published 1994 by Children's Press, Chicago.

Dillon, Richard H. *North American Indian Wars*, Facts on File, Inc., New York, 1983.

Elman, Robert. *Badmen of the West*, Castle Books, Secaucus, New Jersey, 1974.

Fletcher, Maurine, ed. *The Wetherills of the Mesa Verde: Autobiography of Benjamin Alfred Wetherill*, University of Nebraska Press, Lincoln, 1987.

Goetzmann, William H. *Army Exploration in the American West 1803-1863*, University of Nebraska, Lincoln, 1979.

Goetzmann, William H. *Exploration and Empire*, W. W. Norton, New York, 1978.

Goodwin, Vaughn. "'Uncle Dick' Wootton," *Muzzle Blasts Magazine*, Friendship, Indiana, Vol. 52 No. 7, 1991.

Hafen, LeRoy R., ed. "With Fur Traders in Colorado, 1839-40, the Journal of E. Willard Smith," *The Colorado Magazine*, Colorado Historical Society, Denver, July 1950. Reprinted by Territorial Press, Franklin, Tennessee, 1988.

Hales, Peter B. *William Henry Jackson and the Transformation of the American Landscape*, Temple University Press, Philadelphia, 1988.

Haley, J. Evetts. "Charles Goodnight, Pioneer," *The Panhandle-Plains Historical Review*, Canyon, Texas, Vol. 3, 1930.

Hodge, Frederick W., ed. *Handbook of American Indians*, Bureau of American Ethnology, Washington, D.C., 1910.

Horan, James D. *Pictorial History of the Wild West*, Crown Publishers, Inc., New York, 1954.

Hurt, Amy Passmore. "Ouray the Arrow," *Great Indians of the West*, Charlton Publications, Inc., Derby, Connecticut, 1972.

Hutchins, James S. "The Fight at Beecher Island," *Great Western Indian Fights*, University of Nebraska Press, Lincoln, 1960.

Jackson, Clarence S. *Picture Maker of the Old West: William H. Jackson*, Charles Scribner's Sons, New York, 1947.

Kopper, Philip. *The Smithsonian Book of North American Indians Before the Coming of Columbus*, Smithsonian Books, Washington, D.C., 1986.

Lamar, Howard R., ed. "'Buffalo Bill' Cody," *The Reader's Encyclopedia of the American West*, Harper & Row, New York, 1977.

Lamar, Howard R., ed. "The Great Diamond Hoax," *The Reader's Encyclopedia of the American West*, Harper & Row, New York, 1977.

Lebsack, Linda M. *Dr. Nolie Mumey Centennial*, Catalogue No. 5, Linda M. Lebsack Books, Denver, 1991.

Martin, Sharon E. "Fine Place to Visit? You Betchum!" *True West*, Stillwater, Oklahoma, Vol. 39 No. 9, 1992.

Mazzulla, Fred and Jo. *Al Packer: A Colorado Cannibal*, privately printed, Denver, 1968.

O'Neal, Bill. "Clay Allison vs. Charles Faber and Deputies," *True West*, Stillwater, Oklahoma, Vol. 39 No. 9, 1992.

O'Neil, Paul. *The End and the Myth*, Time-Life Books, Alexandria, Virginia, 1979.

Parkman, Francis. *The Oregon Trail*, Little, Brown, and Company, Boston, 1927.

Powell, J. W. *The Exploration of the Colorado River and Its Canyons*, Dover Publications, New York, 1961.

Quaife, Milo Milton, ed. *Kit Carson's Autobiography*, University of Nebraska Press, Lincoln, 1966.

Ruxton, George Frederick. *Life in the Far West*, University of Oklahoma Press, Norman, 1951.

Samuels, Peggy and Harold. *Samuels' Encyclopedia of Artists of the American West*, Castle Books, Secaucus, New Jersey, 1985.

Scott, Hollis J. "LeRoy R. Hafen, 47 Years as Chronicler of Western Americana," *Utah Historical Quarterly*, Utah State Historical Society, Salt Lake City, Vol. 34 No. 3, 1966.

Stegner, Wallace. *Beyond the Hundredth Meridian*, University of Nebraska Press, Lincoln, 1982.

Sunder, John F., ed. *Matt Field on the Santa Fe Trail*, University of Oklahoma Press, Norman, 1960.

Thrapp, Dan L. *Encyclopedia of Frontier Biography*, The Arthur H. Clark Company, Glendale, California, 1988.

Underwood, Larry D. *Guns, Gold & Glory*, Media Publishing, Lincoln, Nebraska, 1992.

Utley, Robert M. *Fort Union National Monument*, National Park Service, U.S. Department of the Interior, Washington, D.C., 1962.

Utley, Robert M., and Washburn, Wilcomb E. *The American Heritage History of the Indian Wars*, American Heritage Publishing Company, New York, 1977.

Voynick, Steve. "Denver's Gold Rush Mint," *True West*, Stillwater, Oklahoma, Vol. 39 No. 5, 1992.

Wallace, Robert. *The Miners*, Time-Life Books, Alexandria, Virginia, 1976.

Wasmund, Laurie Marr. "Inter-Ocean Statesman Barney Ford," *True West*, Stillwater, Oklahoma, Vol. 39 No. 4, 1992.

Wheeler, Keith. *The Townsmen*, Time-Life Books, Alexandria, Virginia, 1975.

Williams, Henry T., ed. *The Pacific Tourist*, Henry T. Williams, Publisher, New York, 1877.

Index

It Happened in *Series from TwoDot Books*

An imprint of Falcon Publishing

TWODOT

Featured in this series are fascinating stories about events that helped shape each state's history. Written in a lively, easy-to-read style, each book features 31-34 stories for history buffs of all ages. Entertaining and informative, each book is 6x9", features b&w illustrations, and is only **$8.95**.

It Happened in Arizona
It Happened in Colorado
It Happened in Montana
It Happened in New Mexico
It Happened in Oregon
It Happened in Southern California
It Happened in Texas
It Happened in Washington

More from TwoDot Books

Bozeman and the Gallatin Valley: A History
Charlie's Trail: The Life and Art of C.M. Russell
Flight of the Dove: The Story of Jeannette Rankin
Growing up Western
Heart of the Trail: The Stories of Eight Wagon Train Women
Jeannette Rankin: Bright Star in the Big Sky
Men with Sand: Great Explorers of the American West
Montana Campfire Tales: Fourteen Historical Essays
More Than Petticoats: Remarkable Montana Women
The Champion Buffalo Hunter
The Only Good Bear is a Dead Bear
Today I Bailed Some Hay to Feed the Sheep the Coyotes Eat

The TwoDot line features classic western literature and history. Each book celebrates and interprets the vast spaces and rich culture of the American West.

FALCON®

To order check with your local bookseller or call Falcon at

1-800-582-2665

Ask for a FREE catalog featuring a complete list of titles on nature, outdoor recreation, travel and the West.